It is said that when the Buddha first had his enlightenment he was asked, "Are you a God?" "No," he replied. "Are you a saint?" "No." "Then what are you?" And he answered, "I am awake."

This waking state is Zen's goal. And over the many centuries of Zen's existence, its masters have perfected ways to awaken—sometimes subtly, sometimes sharply, sometimes quite rudely—those seeking enlightenment.

GAMES ZEN MASTERS PLAY presents these techniques as recorded in the most important Zen texts, with commentaries to aid the Western reader. Its object is not to alter Zen for Western consumption, but to make Zen accessible to the West. In so doing, it takes its place as one of those key works that are making Zen an increasingly potent force throughout the world today.

DR. REGINALD HORACE BLYTH was born in England in 1898, but spent most of his adult life in the Orient, in India, Korea, and Japan. His first book, *Zen in English Literature and Oriental Classics,* was written in Japan while he was interned as an enemy alien during World War II. He remained in Japan after the war, teaching, writing, and translating. By the time of his death in 1964, R. H. Blyth was recognized as one of the leading Western authorities on both Zen and Japanese poetry, as well as being a highly regarded poet in his own right.

More MENTOR Books of Related Interest

GAMES
ZEN MASTERS
PLAY

Writings of R. H. Blyth

SELECTED, EDITED,
AND WITH AN
INTRODUCTION BY ROBERT SOHL
AND AUDREY CARR

A MENTOR BOOK

NEW AMERICAN LIBRARY

NEW YORK AND SCARBOROUGH, ONTARIO

DEDICATED
TO
TOM

Copyright © 1976 by Robert Sohl and Audrey Carr

Library of Congress Catalog Card Number: 75-24786

MENTOR TRADEMARK REG. U.S. PAT. OFF. AND FOREIGN COUNTRIES
REGISTERED TRADEMARK—MARCA REGISTRADA
HECHO EN WINNIPEG, CANADA

SIGNET, SIGNET CLASSIC, MENTOR, PLUME, MERIDIAN AND NAL
BOOKS are published *in the United States* by
New American Library,
1633 Broadway, New York, New York 10019,
in Canada by The New American Library of Canada Limited,
81 Mack Avenue, Scarborough, Ontario M1L 1M8

First Printing, February, 1976

4   5   6   7   8   9   10   11   12

PRINTED IN CANADA

CONTENTS

FOREWORD

With the death of Dr. Reginald Horace Blyth on October 28, 1964, the world lost one of the most eminent exponents of Japanese culture of recent years. His studies on *haiku* and the Japanese sense of humor as well as Zen were unique contributions toward East–West understanding.

Dr. Blyth was born in London in 1898. His earliest contact with the Orient took place in India. However, disapproving of the way some of his countrymen were treating Indian subjects, he moved on to Seoul, Korea, where he taught English at one of the colleges under the Japanese administration in 1924. It was while in Korea that he became interested in Zen Buddhism and studied it under Kayama Taigi Roshi. Ever since, his thoughts were closely connected with Zen, though not always in the orthodox tradition.

He arrived in Japan in 1940, wishing to understand the people and their culture. He settled in Kanazawa, once more as a teacher of English at the Fourth Koto Gakko. But with the outbreak of World War II he was soon interned as an enemy national, and lived in an internment camp near Kobe for about four years. It was during this

1

period of confinement that he devoted himself to writing, finishing his first book, *Zen in English Literature and Oriental Classics* (1942), and parts of the four volumes on *Haiku* (1949).

While in Tokyo he taught at several colleges and universities, including Gakushu-in University and the former Peers' School, and became tutor of English to the Crown Prince.

Dr. Blyth in the meantime never ceased writing assiduously, as his bibliography will show. There appeared more than a dozen titles within the course of ten years: *Senryu* (1950), *Japanese Humour* (1957), *Oriental Humour* (1959), *Zen and Zen Classics*, Vols. I, II, V (1960–4), *Japanese Life and Character in Senryu* (1961), *Edo Satirical Verse Anthologies* (1961), *A History of Haiku*, Vols. I and II (1963–4), and many more. *Zen and Zen Classics* were to have been in eight volumes and promised to be the most complete work on Zen so far to be presented to the English-reading public. The *Hekigan* is among the classics Dr. Blyth had contemplated dealing with. It is regrettable, indeed, that only three volumes could see the light while he lived.

Perhaps to those of us who knew him, he was first and foremost a poet with a wonderfully keen and sensitive perception.

—D. T. Suzuki

INTRODUCTION

The goose is out

THE GAME OF HIDE-AND-SEEK

There is a Hindu myth about the Self or God of the universe who sees life as a form of play. But since the Self is what there is and all that there is and thus has no one separate to play *with*, he plays the cosmic game of hide-and-seek with himself. He takes on the roles and masks of individual people such as you and I and thus becomes involved in exciting and terrifying adventures, all the time forgetting who he really is. Eventually, however, the Self awakens from his many dreams and fantasies and remembers his true identity, the one and eternal Self of the cosmos who is never born and never dies.

Although this is somewhat of a myth in its traditional form, it is a great deal more than this alone. For it symbolizes a universal experience that has permeated nearly every major religion in one form or another and which lies at the root of much of the world's great creativity, whether in literature, philosophy, music, or other forms of expression. It is a dramatic representation of the experience which we in the West have referred to as Cosmic Consciousness. In other cultures it has been described in various ways such as enlightenment, liberation, moksha, Nirvana, satori, and even the Kingdom of Heaven in the terminology of Jesus.

From this ancient Hindu view, we can see society as a kind of play or drama which is being acted out by the central Self of the universe. The Self hides in the roles and personalities of separate individuals until he once again awakens and remembers his true nature. It is precisely this goal of awakening that is the essence of Zen, the universal experience which unmasks the Self behind all the various parts of the great tragic comedy of life.

Zen is neither a religion nor a philosophy, but a way of liberation, a way of disentangling ourselves from the social level of masks and role-playing which we have mistaken for our true identity. For the purpose of Zen is the opening of a "third eye," the eye of insight or enlightenment that cuts through the crust of verbal knowledge and reveals the underlying unity and inseparability of the individual and the universe.

A student once went to a famous Zen master with the following question: "If someone were to ask me a hundred years from now what I thought was your deepest understanding, what should I say?" The Zen master replied, "Tell him I said, 'It is simply This!' "

The Zen method of pointing to higher consciousness teaches us to look at what is right before our eyes—"It is simply This!" It has always been in plain sight from the beginning, and yet, for this very reason it is hard to see. Thus, as the Zen scholar Suzuki put it, "Zen is like looking for the spectacles that are sitting on your nose" or "like looking for an ox when you are riding on the back of it."

Zen teaches, not by words, but by direct pointing, by engaging us in a game or contest with ourselves in which the only answer is a new level of consciousness. Zen is the game of insight, the game of discovering who we are underneath the masks and roles that we call our personality. Normally we assume that our personality is our true self and that the ego is free, independent, and totally different from everyone else. But the object of Zen is to see quite clearly that the personality which we think is our self is a masquerade or a "put-on," a role that is being played out by the universal Self which is the same in each individual.

The word "personality" comes from the Latin word "*persona*," which originally referred to an actor's mask. But just as an actor might play Hamlet overzealously onstage, we usually take our own role in society very seriously, forgetting who we really are. Zen is the insight of seeing through the role we are playing and thus becoming aware of the Self, the real actor behind the mask.

When the Buddha first had his enlightenment, he was asked, "Are you a God?" "No," he replied. "Are you a saint?" "No." "Then what are you?" And he answered, "I am awake."

It is a rather humiliating discovery to realize that all these years of effort and turmoil have been spent in a state of slumber, that from our earliest memories of childhood we have been half asleep and have been acting with only partial awareness. We have been hypnotized by the nature of words, thus becoming alienated from our own organism and from the larger organism of the universe itself.

Rinzai was giving a lecture one day on the "True Man of No Title." A monk, quite perplexed, went up to him and asked, "What is this True Man of No Title?" Rinzai grabbed him by the neck and yelled, "Speak! Speak!" The monk was dumbfounded and could say nothing. Rinzai let go of him and exclaimed: "What worthless stuff is this True Man of No Title!"

The "True Man of No Title" is the true life of our organism which is being lived through us but of which we are largely unconscious. For the hypnosis created by our social conditioning has convinced us that we are some kind of separate agent who is inside the organism controlling it. It is this very illusion of the controller standing back from the organism and the thinker standing apart from the thought process that Zen seeks to dispel.

Freud was obviously on the right track in his claim that all love is basically narcissistic. The only way others can be loved, as he pointed out, is through an expanded narcissism in which one takes them within himself and loves them as himself. Yet he failed to carry this narcissism to its ultimate conclusion in which it would include within itself the whole universe, thus doing away with the separation of the conscious from the unconscious, the subject from the object.

The elimination of the conscious-unconscious dichotomy would resolve every other dichotomy as well; for the world appears as an object external to oneself only to the extent that one has accepted unconsciously the "persona" or social role that has been thrust upon one by society. Such a realization as this, not only on an intellectual level but at the very center of one's consciousness, would seem to precede the strange revelation described below.

"One day I wiped out all the notions from my mind. I gave up all desire. I discarded all the words with which I thought and stayed in quietude. I felt a little queer—as if I were being carried into something, or as if I were touching some power unknown to me . . . and Ztt! I entered. I lost the boundary of my physical body. I had my skin, of course, but I felt I was standing in the center of the cosmos. I spoke, but my words had lost their meaning. I saw people coming toward me, but all were the same man. All were myself! I had never known this world. I had believed that I was created, but now I must change my opinion: I was never created; I was the cosmos; no individual Mr. Sasaki existed."

Through confusing words and abstractions with reality itself, we have created an artificial role or personality for ourselves and in the process forgotten that it is just a role and not the real source of our actions. Society has tricked us into the belief that our minds are inside our heads and act independently from it at the same time that it is also telling us who we are and what we should be doing. But since the mind then includes all of one's social relationships, it is not inside the skin of the individual at all but is actually outside of it.

"And that," as Alan Watts points out, "is just the paradox of the situation; society gives us the idea that the mind, or ego, is inside the skin and that it acts on its own, apart from society. Here, then, is a major contradiction in the rules of the social game. The members of the game are to play *as if* they were independent agents, but they are not to *know* that they are just playing as if! It is explicit in the rules that the individual is self-determining, but implicit that he is so only by virtue of the rules. Furthermore, while he is defined as an independent agent, he must not be so independent as not to submit to the rules which define him. Thus he is defined as an agent in order to be held responsible to the group for "his" actions. The rules of the game confer independence and take it away at the same time without revealing the contradiction."

The ego-contradiction is the basic thorn which society has implanted since childhood and from which we are suffering without being able to see the vicious circle involved. We have been convinced that we are free and independent agents and yet, the very agent referred to is actually a social role that is defined by other people and has no real freedom to act at all.

When beginning to understand the trap involved, the usual question is to ask what one should do to get out of it. And here is where Zen is rather ingenious. For we are told to "do" nothing to get out of it since the very "doing" will only be another level of the same contradiction that one is trying to see through. Instead of "doing," or for that matter "not doing," we need a kind of passive awareness of ourselves in every situation. For only awareness, NOW, in the present moment can reveal the true source of action, which is not the ego at all but rather the total environmental field of which the organism is only one side of a mutual polarity.

GAMES ZEN MASTERS PLAY

Yungchia walked round the Sixth Patriarch three times without bowing and merely shook his Buddhist staff with iron rings. The Patriarch said, "A Sramana embodies the 3,000 rules of deportment and the 80,000 minute moral rules. From whence does your honor come, may I ask, with your overweening self-assurance?" Yungchia replied, "Birth-and-death is a problem of great moment; all changes ceaselessly." Huineng asked, "Why not embody impermanence, and so solve it?" Yungchia replied, "To be unborn and deathless is to embody it; to be timeless is to solve it." "That is so, that is so," assented the Patriarch. At this, Yungchia acted according to the prescribed ceremonial and prostrated himself, then soon after bade farewell to the Patriarch. "Aren't you in a bit of a hurry to be off?" said the Patriarch, but Yungchia retorted, "Motion has no real existence, so how can there be such a thing as 'hurry'?" "Who knows that motion is unreal?" "You yourself are discriminating in asking such a question." The Patriarch exclaimed, "You have grasped birthlessness splendidly!" but Yungchia remarked, "Has the expression 'birthlessness' any meaning whatever?" The Patriarch countered with, "If it had no meaning, how could anybody discriminate?" "Discrimination is meaning!" asserted

Yungchia "Very good indeed!" exclaimed the Patriarch.

This is a splendid example of the games Zen masters play, the type of attack and counterattack that one encounters in the literature of Zen Buddhism. That the West has discovered Zen in the twentieth century may, in retrospect, turn out to be one of the most significant developments of our time. Starting with the Buddha's enlightenment in the fifth century before Christ, it was a thousand years later that the blue-eyed monk Bodhidharma carried the wordless teaching to China. And today, after a period of another fifteen centuries, a similar feat has been performed by the Japanese Zen scholar Daisetz T. Suzuki.

Suzuki did such an amazing job of presenting Zen to the West that during the fifties and sixties he lived to see the tremendous growth of interest in Zen all over the world. Philosophers, theologians, psychiatrists, poets, artists, and others from many different disciplines have seen in Zen many of the missing links in their own work, and out of this interplay a truly Western form of Zen is gradually emerging. Perhaps a good place to pursue our quest for the inner key to this ancient Oriental tradition is to ask Suzuki himself: "Please tell us, Dr. Suzuki, in as few words as possible, what Zen is."

"The truth is, Zen is extremely elusive as far as its outward aspects are concerned; when you think you have caught a glimpse of it, it is no more there; from afar it looks so approachable, but as soon as you come near it you see it even further away from you than before."

Suzuki, obviously, was a truly great master of the game. And the answer which he has given us is not too different from the famous story of Rinzai, who kept going to his teacher Obaku to learn the secret of Zen and each time had the gate slammed in his face. This is part of the game itself, to make it as difficult as possible to get in on the secret, thus making one even more intent on getting to the bottom of it. Rinzai, in fact, went back again, and this time when the gate slammed in his face his leg got caught in it and was broken. However, it was from the very pain which he suffered that he had a realization and saw into the secret of Zen which he had been seeking for many years.

Baso used to sit cross-legged from morning till night in constant meditation. His master Nangaku saw him and asked: "Why are you sitting cross-legged in meditation?" "I am trying to become a Buddha," he answered. The master picked up a brick and began polishing it on a stone nearby. "What are you doing, Master?" asked Baso. "I am trying to turn this brick into a mirror," was the answer. "No amount of polishing will turn the brick into a mirror, sir." "If so, no amount of sitting cross-legged will make you into a Buddha," retorted the master.

Nangaku's point is not that there is anything inherently wrong with sitting cross-legged, but that the idea of becoming a Buddha is still based on a division between present and future, between ourselves and something else which stands apart from us. It is this very type of thinking based on an illusory separation of subject and object which traps us in a vicious circle of goals, never realizing that we are already one with the universe and therefore have nothing outside of ourselves to be gained.

Zen is the very essence of life itself, the merging of opposites in which man merges with the universe and realizes his true identity. We live supposedly in a world of opposites, of white against black, of here versus there. But beneath this level of opposition lies a sea of tranquility in which all things are complementary rather than contradictory.

> On the sea of death and life,
>   the diver's boat is freighted
>   With "Is" and "Is not";
>   But if the bottom is broken through,
>   "Is" and "Is not" disappear.

When the bottom is broken through and "Is" and "Is not" disappear, there is still something which remains, however difficult it may be to define. Thus we are told that before we study Zen the mountains are mountains and the rivers are rivers. While we are studying Zen, however, the mountains are no longer mountains and the rivers no longer rivers. But then when our study of Zen is completed, the mountains are once again mountains and the rivers once again rivers.

When a Zen master explained this to one of his students, the student exclaimed: "Well, if that is true, then there is no difference between the ordinary man and the enlightened man." "That's true," replied the master. "There is no difference, really. The only thing is, the enlightened man is six inches off the ground!"

One day Hyakujo was out taking a walk with his master Baso when a flock of wild geese flew overhead. "What are they?" Baso asked. "They are wild geese." "Where are they flying?" "They have already flown away, Master." At this point in the game, Baso suddenly grabbed Hyakujo's nose and twisted it until, overcome by pain, Hyakujo cried out, "Oh, oh!" "You say they have flown away," said Baso, "but really they have been here from the very beginning."

Hyakujo's statement "they have flown away" is true enough on the ordinary level of common sense. They are no longer here but have gone someplace else. But at the moment of acute pain his normal thinking process was stopped and he saw directly what Baso was pointing to in his statement "they have been here from the very beginning." The point of the statement is not a new kind of logic or belief but a new way of seeing which Zen calls the opening of the third eye. Zen is an "open secret" which has been right in front of our eyes from the very beginning. As it is stated in the *Zenrin Kushu:*

> Nothing whatever is hidden;
> From of old, all is clear as daylight.

To confuse the indivisible nature of reality with the differentiations and conceptual pigeonholes of language is the basic ignorance from which Zen seeks to free us. The ultimate answers to existence are not to be found in intellectual concepts and philosophies, however sophisticated, but rather in a level of direct nonconceptual experience which can never be limited to the dualistic nature of language. Asked how Zen could be taught if this were so, one master answered that it was somewhat like learning the art of burglary.

The son of a burglar saw his father growing older and thought: "If he is unable to carry out his profession, who will be the breadwinner of this family, except myself? I must learn the trade." He intimated the idea to his father, who approved of it. One night the father took the son to a big house, broke through the fence, entered the house, and opening one of the large chests, told the son to go in and pick out the clothings. As soon as he got into it, the lid was dropped and the lock securely applied. The father now came out to the courtyard and, loudly knocking at the door, woke up the whole family, whereas he himself quietly slipped away by the former hole in the fence. The residents got excited and lighted candles, but found that the burglars had already gone. The son, who remained all the time in the chest securely confined, thought of his cruel father. He was greatly mortified, when a fine idea flashed upon him. He made a noise which sounded like the gnawing of a rat. The family told the maid to take a candle and examine the chest. When the lid was unlocked, out came the prisoner, who blew out the light, pushed away the maid, and fled. The people ran after him. Noticing a well by the road, he picked up a large stone and threw it into the water. The pursuers all gathered around the well, trying to find the burglar drowning himself in the dark hole. In the meantime he was safely back in his father's house. He blamed the latter very much for his narrow escape. Said the father: "Be not offended, my son. Just tell me how you got off." When the son told him all about his adventures, the father remarked, "There you are, you have learned the art!"

THE GOOSE IS OUT

A monk said to Seijo: "I am told that a Buddha who lived in ancient times sat in meditation for ten cycles of existence and still could not realize the truth of liberation. Why was this so?"

Seijo answered him, "Your question is self-explanatory."

Again, the monk persisted. "Since the Buddha meditated, why couldn't he attain Buddhahood?"

Seijo replied: "Because he was not a Buddha."

While Buddhism in its Indian form was a rather serious logical exercise in seeing the illusion of selfhood, the Chinese added a humor and love of paradox that have become the trademark of Zen. For the method of Zen, if one could call it a method, is to see that everything is quite self-explanatory and that it is only we ourselves who are intent on making a problem out of it. We are too easily taken in by words and abstractions which create various kinds of false problems that are not real but only conceptual.

Such a discovery is particularly difficult for a

Westerner to comprehend, raised as we have been on thinkers such as the famous Frenchman Descartes, who based his philosophy on the one premise he believed undoubtable: *"Cogito ergo sum*—I think, therefore I am."* To a Westerner this must indeed sound self-evident, as it did to Descartes. Much of Western philosophy and religion is based on this very premise, that there is a permanent thinker behind the thought process who persists through time and who we refer to when we use the word "I."

It comes, therefore, as somewhat of a surprise when we read such Eastern sages as Krishnamurti telling us that the "I" is unreal, that there is not really a thinker who is creating our thoughts. And yet, strangely enough, this is also the message which the Zen masters have sought to communicate through all of their eccentric behavior and paradoxical sayings. Life is a unitary process which we learn to divide into subject and object and then spend our lives worrying over how to get it back together. Thus when we ask the master for instructions on how to be liberated, he tells us to find out *who* it is that is asking the question.

A monk asked Joshu, "What is the Buddha?" "The one in the Hall." The monk said, "The one in the Hall is a statue, a lump of mud!" Joshu said, "That is so." "What is the Buddha?" asked the monk. "The one in the Hall."

The masters make use of a great variety of tricks and traps to force the student to see how ridiculous is his question. For the answer is usually in the question itself and not something apart from it, which in Zen terminology would be like adding legs to a painted snake. The answer is one of perception rather than words, which was why one Zen master replied, "When you know the answer you won't ask the question." Thus a monk asked Gensha, "The Supreme Doctrine—is there any explanation of it recently?" Gensha said, "We don't hear such a thing often."

We don't hear Zen explained very often. However, this is not because it is too difficult to explain but because there is really nothing to say. R. H. Blyth, whose profound insights into Zen are contained in this book, has expressed the point in the following way:

"I have been asked many questions in my life about poetry, religion, life, and I have given precisely the same number of answers, but I have never, I repeat, *never*, satisfied a single interlocutor. Why was this? Because all questioning is a way of avoiding the real answer, which, as Zen tells us, is really known already. Every man is enlightened, but wishes he wasn't. Every man knows he must love his enemies, and sell all he has and give to the poor, but he doesn't wish to know it—so he asks questions."

A military man went to the master Nansen with the following problem: "A man once kept a goose in a bottle, feeding it until it grew too large to get through the bottleneck. Now, how did he get the goose out without killing it or breaking the bottle?" The master said to him, "Oh, officer?" to which he replied, "Yes, Master?" and the master exclaimed: "There! The goose is out of the bottle!"

The most obvious thing, of course, is that the real problem was never one of getting the goose out of the bottle but rather of getting ourselves out of it. For the bottleneck life imposes is our normal conditioned way of seeing things, in which we confront them as alien objects that stand in our way rather than as an extension of our own consciousness. This is the real secret of Zen and the point of all of its paradoxes and strange-sounding contradictions. We had been taught to believe that the mind was inside of us and that all of our perceptions of the world were outside. But from the Zen point of view, it is just the opposite. The mind is really outside and all of our perceptions are inside of It. Or to put it another way, "The goose is out!"

Wittgenstein stated that he did not solve philosophical problems, he dissolved them. "He asks himself, 'What is your aim in philosophy?' and he answers, 'To show the fly the way out of the fly-bottle.' And where is he when he has made his escape? He is, it appears, exactly where he started; for philosophy 'leaves everything as it is.' The point that Wittgenstein had in mind was that it was not the business of philosophy to add to our information, nor yet to alter our language; it makes no difference of this sort. But it does make a difference in that by it we may achieve a clear view, a grasp, a command of what was indeed always there to be seen, but had not before been seen in all its bearings and connections. We leave things as they are; but perhaps for the first time we come to see them as they are."

If this is indeed the point of Wittgenstein's philosophizing, it is also the point of all the Zen stories. "We leave things as they are; but perhaps for

the first time we come to see them as they are."
Kipling's statement to the contrary, it may be that
the dualism of East and West is to be transcended
like every other dualism. For we find an increasing
number of creative people, trained and raised in
the traditions of Western science, and yet speaking
in terms that sound strangely reminiscent of the
ancient East. An eloquent example can be seen in
the words of one of America's leading psychoan-
alysts, Erich Fromm.

"If one pursues the aim of the full recovery of
the unconscious, then this task is not restricted to
the instincts, nor to other limited sectors of experience, but to the total experience of the total man;
then the aim becomes that of overcoming alienation, and of the subject-object split in perceiving
the world; it means the de-repression, the aboli-
tion of the split within myself between the universal man and the social man; it means giving up the
illusion of an indestructible separate ego, which is
to be enlarged and preserved, as the Egyptian
pharaohs hoped to preserve themselves as mum-
mies for eternity. To be conscious of the unconscious means to be open, responding, 'to have'
nothing and to be."

A new day is emerging in religion and philosophy, a day in which the differences and divergen-
cies of many schools and sects can be seen in the
light of a greater unity. The great mystics of
Catholicism and the Protestant death-of-god theologians; the existentialist philosophers and the
students of linguistic analysis; the depth psycholo-
gies of Jung and Freud and the ancient wisdom of
Hinduism and Buddhism: these are some of the

major schools and movements in the new world of philosophy, a world that is transcending its limited views and partialities and discovering the essential unity that underlies such great diversity.

The Absolute of Hegel, the Tao of Lao-tzu, and the Emptiness or Suchness of Mahayana Buddhism: all are terms for the One that transcends one and many, the all-pervasive unity that contains a universe of differentiations. As the Zen master told his student, "Tell him I said, 'It is simply This'." "Well, then, what is This?" one may ask, "and how does one realize it?" No one has expressed it more clearly than the great teacher of our time, Krishnamurti:

"The establishment of inner harmony is to be attained neither in the past nor in the future, but where the past and the future meet, which is the now. When you have attained that point, neither future nor past, neither birth nor death, neither time nor space exist. It is that NOW which is liberation, which is perfect harmony, to which the men of the past and the men of the future must come."

Assuming that human nature is potentially Buddha-nature, the Enlightenment experience as Asia's greatest gift need not be confined to a single geographical area. The day has finally arrived when Western man, long locked in his ego, and deluded by the shadows on the wall of the cave, can say with his Eastern brother:

> Misty rain on Mount Lu,
> And Waves in Che-chiang;
> When you have not yet been there,
> Many a regret surely you have;

But once there and homeward you wend,
How matter-of-fact things look!
Misty rain on Mount Lu,
And waves surging in Che-chiang.

ROBERT SOHL
AUDREY CARR

1. BASIC
STRATEGY

**The classic Hsinhsinming
translated with commentary**

THERE IS NOTHING DIFFICULT ABOUT THE GREAT WAY, BUT, AVOID CHOOSING!

We suffer, at one and the same time, from excessive pride and excessive humility. On the one hand, our intellect rushes in where angels fear to tread. On the other hand, we are too humble before the Buddhas and saints, not realizing that we too are the Buddha, as the *Avatamsaka (Kegonkyo)* declares:

> *The mind, the Buddha, living creatures—these are not three different things.*

Sengtsan attributes all our uneasiness, our dissatisfaction with ourselves and other people, our inability to understand why we are alive at all, to one great cause: choosing this and rejecting that, clinging to the one and loathing the other. There is a profound saying:

> *The flowers fall, for all our yearning;*
> *Grasses grow, regardless of our dislike.*

ONLY WHEN YOU NEITHER LOVE NOR HATE DOES IT APPEAR IN ALL CLARITY.

There is love and Love, but only hate; there is no such thing as Hate. In Love is included that which might be called Hate, what Lawrence calls "the dark side of love." Insofar as we love, in the sense of being attached to a thing, we hate. Insofar as we Love, whether it be with pain or joy, the Way is walked in by us, we are the Way. Ryoto, a pupil of Basho, says:

> Yield to the willow
> All the loathing,
> All the desire of your heart.

A HAIR'S BREADTH OF DEVIATION FROM IT, AND A DEEP GULF IS SET BETWEEN HEAVEN AND EARTH.

A miss is as good as a mile. The slightest thought of self, that is, by self, and the Great Way is irretrievably lost. A drop of ink, and a glass of clear water is all clouded. Once we think, "This flower is blooming for me; this insect is a hateful nuisance and nothing else; that man is a useless rascal; that woman is a good mother, and she must therefore be a good wife"—when such thoughts arise in our minds, all the cohesion between things disappears; they rattle about in a meaningless and irritating way. Instead of being united into a whole by virtue of their own interpenetrated suchness, they are pulled hither and thither by our arbitrary and ever-changing preferences, our whims and prejudices. We suppose this particular man to be a Buddha, ourselves to be ordinary people, this action to be charming, that to be odious, and fail to see how "All things work together for good." In actual fact, Heaven and Earth cannot be separated; one cannot exist without the other. Together they are the Great Way.

IF YOU WANT TO GET HOLD OF WHAT IT LOOKS LIKE, DO NOT BE ANTI- OR PRO- ANYTHING.

Since the Great Way is one, it is impossible for us to be for this, and aiding that which needs no aid. There is a certain current, a Flow of the universe. We may swim with it or against it, float in the middle of the stream or stagnate in a backwater, but nothing we can do will accelerate or retard that Flow. Yet this Flow is not something separate from ourselves; it is our own flowing; we are not corks bobbing up and down on a stream of inevitability.

THE CONFLICT OF LONGING AND LOATHING— THIS IS THE DISEASE OF THE MIND.

Something arises which pleases the mind, which fits in with our notion of what is profitable for us—and we love it. Something arises which thwarts us, which conflicts with our wants, and we hate it. So long as we possess this individual mind, enlightenment and delusion, pain and pleasure, accepting and rejecting, good and bad toss us up and down on the waves of existence, never moving onward, always the same restlessness and wobbling, the same fear of woe and insecurity of joy. So Wordsworth says, in the *Ode to Duty*:

> *My hopes must no more change their name.*

In addition, the mirror of our mind being distorted, nothing appears in its natural, its original form. The louse appears a dirty, loathsome thing, the lion a noble creature. But when we see the louse as it really is, it is not a merely neutral thing; it is something to be accepted as inevitable in our mortal life, as in Basho's verse:

> *Fleas, lice,*
> *The horse pissing*
> *By my pillow.*

NOT KNOWING THE PROFOUND MEANING OF THINGS, WE DISTURB OUR (ORIGINAL) PEACE OF MIND TO NO PURPOSE.

When we are in the Way, when we act without love or hate, hope or despair or indifference, the meaning of things is self-evident, not merely impossible but unnecessary to express. Conversely, while we are looking for the significance of things, it is nonexistent. Our original nature is one of perfect harmony with the universe, a harmony not of similarity or correspondence but of identity. The *Tsaikentan (Saikontan)* says:

> *The mind that is free from itself—why should it look within? This introspection taught by Buddha only increases the obstruction. Things are originally one; why then should we endeavor to untie them? Chuangtse preaches the identity of contraries, thus dividing up that unity.*

PERFECT LIKE GREAT SPACE, THE WAY HAS NOTHING LACKING, NOTHING IN EXCESS.

Without beginning, without end, without increase or decrease, the Great Way is perfect, like a circle, with nothing too small in the smallest thing, nothing too large in the largest. And this perfection in the dewdrop and in the solar system we are enabled to see, we are driven to see, by the perfection in ourselves. Beyond all this confusion and asymmetry there is a deep harmony and proportion without us and within us that satisfies us when we submit to it, when we take it as it is, but can never be perceived or conceived intellectually.

TRULY, BECAUSE OF OUR ACCEPTING AND REJECTING, WE HAVE NOT THE SUCHNESS OF THINGS.

Our state of mind is not to be fatalistic, saying of bad things, "It can't be helped," and of good things, "What difference does it make?" It must be to want what the universe wants, in the way it wants it, in that place, at that time. This wanting *is* the Way, the wanting *is* the suchness of things; there is no Way, no suchness apart from it.

The suchness of things is what the poet is looking for, listening to, smelling, and tasting. And insofar as he and we listen and touch and see, the suchness has an existence, a meaning, a value. Unless we taste the world, it is tasteless; it is void of suchness. But this tasting is not to be a choosing, tasting some and not tasting others.

NEITHER FOLLOW AFTER, NOR DWELL WITH THE DOCTRINE OF THE VOID.

We are not to be beguiled by the senses, by the apparent differences of things.

> *Rain, hail and snow,*
> *Ice too, are set apart,*
> *But when they fall—*
> *The same water*
> *Of the valley stream.*

On the other hand, we are not to fall into the opposite error of taking all things as unreal and meaningless. Both these extreme views are wrong; Yungchia describes the position in the following way:

> *Getting rid of things and clinging to emptiness*
> *Is an illness of the same kind;*

It is just like throwing oneself into a fire
  To avoid being drowned.

IF THE MIND IS AT PEACE, THESE WRONG VIEWS DISAPPEAR OF THEMSELVES.

Dogen has a waka:

> *Ever the same,*
> *Unchanged of hue,*
>   *Cherry blossoms*
> *Of my native place:*
> *Spring now has gone.*

Here the eternal and the temporal, the unchanged and changing are one, because the flowers are allowed to be the same color as always; they are allowed to fall as always. The flowers are not separated, in their blooming and in their falling, from the poet himself, but neither is it a dream world, an unreal world where all is vanity. It is a world of form and color, of change and decay, yet it is beyond time and place, a world of truth.

WHEN ACTIVITY IS STOPPED AND THERE IS PASSIVITY, THIS PASSIVITY IS A STATE OF ACTIVITY.

The modern theories of repression may be taken as an example of the meaning of this verse. When we thwart nature, suppress our instincts, control our deisres, the energy thus restricted and yet augmented is still active, and may at any time burst forth with volcanic force in some unsuspected direction ... there must be what Wordsworth calls "a wise passiveness," that is, an active rest, such as we find described in the following haiku:

> *I came to the flowers;*
> *I slept beneath them;*
> *This was my leisure.*
>
> —Buson

REMAINING IN MOVEMENT OR QUIESCENCE, HOW SHALL YOU KNOW THE ONE?

Not only movement and quiescence but enlightenment and illusion, life and death and Nirvana, salvation and damnation, profit and loss, this and that—all these are our lot and portion from moment to moment, if we do not realize that the Great Way is one and indivisible however we delude ourselves that we have divided it.

NOT THOROUGHLY UNDERSTANDING THE UNITY OF THE WAY, BOTH (ACTIVITY AND QUIESCENCE) ARE FAILURES.

In other words, mere activity, activity without quiescence, mere quiescence without its inner activity, are no good, neither has its proper quality and function. Freedom is impossible without law, man is nothing without God, illusion nonexistent except for enlightenment, this is this because that is that. But freedom and law, illusion and enlightenment, this and that are two names of one thing. Unless this is realized (in practical life), none of these is its real self. This is not this until and unless it is that; only when the two are one are they really two.

In practical life, this means that the composure we feel at home among our family is only an illusion that is broken when we go out into the world and meet with vexation and disappointment, becoming irritated and depressed. Our activity when playing chess is not the true activity, as we see when we are beaten and our opponent's face and voice become hateful to us. It lacks the balance that preserves the mind from spite though we properly enough feel gloomy at losing.

> IF YOU GET RID OF PHENOMENA, ALL THINGS
> ARE LOST: IF YOU FOLLOW AFTER THE VOID,
> YOU TURN YOUR BACK ON THE SELFLESSNESS
> OF THINGS.

If we suppose that all things are illusions, that everything is meaningless in the ordinary sense of the word, we are misunderstanding the doctrine that all is mind, and losing our grasp on the reality outside us. The difficulty is to hold firmly in the mind the two contradictory elements.

In the early morning we walk out into the garden and see a spider finishing its web. With skill and assiduity all is completed, and it sits in the center, a thing of beauty with its duns and deep blues of arabesque designs. A butterfly flits by, drops too low, and is immediately struggling in the mesh. The spider, though not hungry, approaches, seizes it in his jaws, and poisons it. He returns to the center of the web, leaving a mangled creature for a future meal. A nation conquers the then known world and organizes it with intelligence and ability; a great man appears, is caught and nailed on a cross, a spectacle for all ages and generations. These two examples are identical, despite the addition of intelligence, morality, and religion to the second. Both are to be seen in exactly the same way though with differing degrees of intensity. Whether your children are killed by God (alias an earthquake) or by God (alias a robber) or by God (alias old age), the killing is to be received in the same way. One's attitude to the earthquake and to the robber as such is different, since these two things are intrinsically different.

THE MORE TALKING AND THINKING, THE FARTHER FROM THE TRUTH.

Haiku are the briefest kind of poetry consonant with the possession of form and rhythm. By the reduction of poetical expression to seventeen syllables we narrow the circle around that invisible, unwritable central poetic life until no mistake is possible, no discoloration of the object is left, all is transparent and as though wordless.

CUTTING OFF ALL SPEECH, ALL THOUGHT, THERE IS NOWHERE THAT YOU CANNOT GO.

This does not mean that there is to be no speech, no words, but that there is to be speech that is nonspeaking, silence that is expressive; thought that is ego-less, mindlessness through which Mind is flowing. This mindless, speechless, thinking and talking state is one in which we realize the impermanence of all things. This "realize" does not mean an intellectual comprehension, but a "making real" in ourselves an actual-potential state. It is not that all things are impermanent and that we must perceive this fact, but that our "seeing" the change that a thing is, and the change that is seen are one activity, neither cause nor effect, neither hen nor egg.

"There is nowhere that you cannot go," in other words, you are Buddha—not *a* Buddha, but *the* Buddha, beyond all time and space, eternal and infinite, yet here and now. You have all because you have nothing; having no desires they are all fulfilled, yet you own property; you hope for this and that, talk and think, plan and daydream.

RETURNING TO THE ROOT, WE GET THE ESSENCE: FOLLOWING AFTER APPEARANCES WE LOSE THE SPIRIT.

What is the "root" of the universe? Some say man, some say God. It is often convenient to have two names for one thing: spiritual, material; human, divine; free will, determinism; relative, absolute. But if we think of the essence of things as the root, and the things themselves as branches and leaves, we are allowing these "thoughts" and "words," spoken of in the previous verse, to divide once more what is a living unity into a duality that is dead as such. For whether we look at things in their multifariousness, their variety and differences, or at the common elements, the "Life-force," the principles of Science, we are still far from the root, which is not either, not both, not a thing at all—yet it is not nothing. Buddhists say the mind is the root of things—but it is not something inside us. Christians say it is God—but it is not something outside us. But to know, to *realize*, the inside and outside as one, that my profit is your profit, that your loss is my loss, to make this fact, this dead matter-of-fact into a living, yea-saying Fact—this is our own and our only problem. When this is solved, in our thinking and speaking, all is solved. When it is not solved, every thought is twisted, every word is sophisticated. Yungchia uses the same metaphor of root and leaves in the following verse:

Cutting off the root (of life and death) directly,
This is the mark of Buddhahood;

If you go on plucking leaves (of creeds) and seek-
ing branches (of abstract principles),
I can do nothing for you.

**IF FOR ONLY A MOMENT WE SEE WITHIN,
WE HAVE SURPASSED THE EMPTINESS
OF THINGS.**

Moments of vision, provided that we are watchful for and unforgetful of them, coming and going as they do like a breath of air, enable us to go beyond the transitoriness, the emptiness, the unreality of things—into what? Our going is to nowhere, our going is staying here. It is the timeless and spaceless that cannot exist except in time and space. What happiness to have so many of these moments, for them to run in a stream through our lives! Nietzsche, Mozart, Spinoza, Marcus Aurelius, Basho—this is what these names mean to us, the painful happiness of these moments of seeing within.

**CHANGES THAT GO ON IN THIS EMPTINESS
ALL APPEAR BECAUSE OF OUR IGNORANCE.**

Once we realize that there is no such thing as reality, nothing can appear as real or unreal. All things are empty in their self-nature, and when we realize that nothing is unreal, we are at home in every place; every moment of time, whether past or present, is now. In our regrets for what is past, time lives in eternity. Our thoughts wander through infinite space, which is thus in this point of feeling matter.

DO NOT SEEK FOR THE TRUTH, ONLY STOP HAVING AN OPINION.

The drowning man searches for water. A more homely and apt illustration is a man looking for the spectacles that are on his nose. Confucius says, "making an axe, looking at the one you are using." There is no such thing as "the Truth." The nearest approach to anything like it is our state of mind when we desist from the search for it, and live our life. This is what the *Sutra of Perfect Enlightenment* means when it says:

> *Positive views are all perverted views;*
> *All no-opinions are true opinions.*

And Yungchia says also explicitly,

> *Do not seek for the truth,*
> *Do not cut off delusions.*

DO NOT REMAIN IN THE RELATIVE VIEW OF THINGS; RELIGIOUSLY AVOID FOLLOWING IT.

In every way the world is double, good and bad, profit and loss, here and there. But from another

40

point of view, "There is nothing good or bad but thinking makes it so." We are to stop this "thinking," this "having an opinion," this "judging." Yet if we say, this is the right view, this is the wrong, this the relative, this is the absolute, we are still "following" it. Truth is attained only when we realize that there is nothing to attain to. Eternity has its fullness of perfection in us only when we are engrossed in the temporal and imperfect.

IF THERE IS THE SLIGHTEST TRACE OF THIS AND THAT, THE MIND IS LOST IN A MAZE OF COMPLEXITY.

The Middle Way is indeed a difficult path to tread, a razor-edge from which we fall into the common errors of mankind. When we compare the Chinese above with the Hebrew,

Thou shalt worship no other God; for the Lord, whose name is Jealous, is a jealous God,

we cannot but be struck by the variety of expressions of an identical, inexpressible truth. There is here a variety in which the Mind is *not* lost; this *is* that, however well disguised.

DUALITY ARISES FROM UNITY;
BUT DO NOT BE ATTACHED TO THIS UNITY.

It is the One that unites the Two; without It, the Buddha-Nature, the Void, the Mind, this and that could not exist. But do not despise this and that and yearn after the Ground of Existence. Things and circumstances are in themselves neutral, not meaningless, but *not* colored intrinsically with the "opinions" we have of them.

> *When we clap our hands,*
> *The maid serves tea,*
>   *Birds fly up,*
> *Fish draw near—*
> *At the pond in Sarusawa.*

The clapping of the hands is It. The sound as interpreted by the maidservant, by the bird, by the fish is only half of It. But without halves there is no whole, just as without a whole there are no halves. As we endeavor to release ourselves from phenomena, the relative world, we become attached to something even more nonexistent, the thing in itself, the noumenon, and thus also it is said,

> *Holding to the One is not Truth.*

**WHEN THE MIND IS ONE, AND NOTHING
HAPPENS, EVERYTHING IN THE WORLD
IS UNBLAMABLE.**

"Nothing happens" means our realizing that nothing increases or decreases, things are as they are. This is "realized" when the mind is undivided, when in my own person you and I, he and I are different names of one thing, that is nevertheless two things. When nothing in the world is "blamed" as itself and nothing else, or as everything, when, that is, nature has done its part and we do ours, when we do not upbraid circumstances or indulge in self-reproach, the mind is the mind and nothing untoward can occur. Chesterton rightly says,

*An adventure is only an inconvenience rightly
    understood.
An inconvenience is only an adventure wrongly
    considered.*

**IF THINGS ARE UNBLAMED, THEY CEASE TO
EXIST; IF NOTHING HAPPENS, THERE IS
NO MIND.**

When we neither censure nor praise anything, all things are devoid of censurable and praiseworthy qualities. When we do not judge things, things do not judge us. When things simply flow, every atom according to its nature, according to Nature, according to its Buddha nature, there is no mind as something separate from what is not mind. Yungchia says:

Walking is Zen, sitting is Zen;
Whether we speak or are silent, move or are still,
It is unperturbed.

WHEN THINGS CEASE TO EXIST, THE MIND FOLLOWS THEM: WHEN THE MIND VANISHES, THINGS ALSO FOLLOW IT.

Subject and object, I and that, here and there—when one or the other (it does not matter which) ceases, both cease. According to our temperaments, we find it less difficult to become aware of the emptiness of the ego-concept or the emptiness of the thing-concept. It is the same difference that gives us the *jiriki* and *tariki* sects, self-power and other-power. The first line refers to the former, and the second to the latter. Yungchia says:

Trying to get rid of illusion, and seeking to grasp reality—
This giving up and keeping is mere sophistry and lies.

In other words, seeking for the truth and avoiding discrimination is itself discrimination. So long as we look for reality outside ourselves, or inside ourselves, so long will things refrain from following the (non-) ego into nonexistence, and the (illusory) ego refrain from following things into their emptiness. Outside and inside are the same thing.

44

THINGS ARE THINGS BECAUSE OF THE MIND; THE MIND IS THE MIND BECAUSE OF THINGS.

The aim of Zen, the aim of the poetical life, is to reach and remain in that undifferentiated state where subject and object are one, in which the object is perceived by simple introspection, the subject is a self-conscious object. Subject and object are to be realized as the two sides of one sheet of paper, that is one and yet is two. The one piece of paper cannot exist without the two sides, nor the two sides without the one sheet. This analogy fails to satisfy if taken in any other way but lightly and quickly, for to what should we compare the universe? How can anything be a true parable of the Essence of Being?

IF YOU WISH TO KNOW WHAT THESE TWO ARE, THEY ARE ORIGINALLY ONE EMPTINESS.

This Emptiness is described in the following way: it is perfectly Harmonious, subject and object, Mind and Form are one. It is Pure and Undefiled; things are, just as they are, delivered from all stain of sin or imperfection. It is Unobstructed; all things are free, interpenetrative. That is to say, it is ageless, nonmoral, lawless. It is like light, containing all colors in it, but itself colorless. It is not a thing but contains all things; not a person but includes all minds; not beautiful or ugly but the essence of both.

IN THIS VOID, BOTH (MIND AND THINGS) ARE ONE, ALL THE MYRIAD PHENOMENA CONTAINED IN BOTH.

All mental phenomena are contained in things; all things are contained in the mind. But this "in" has an interpenetrative meaning; it is not the "in" of "inside" and "outside." An example of this interpenetration:

> *The Rose of Sharon*
> *At the side of the road*
> *Was eaten by my horse.*

—Basho

IF YOU DO NOT DISTINGUISH "REFINED" AND "COARSE," HOW CAN YOU BE *for* THIS AND *against* THAT?

By "refined" and "coarse" is meant all the pairs of relatives under which we look at the world. Habit makes it seem a necessity that we should view the world so, since custom lies upon us "with a weight heavy as frost, and deep almost as life," but moments of vision, all moments profound enough to reach through to the Void, the Ground of Being, the Way, tell us that refined or coarse though things be, they are something which is neither, yet which is not neither. Thoreau gives us an example, all the truer because it is an unconscious one, of the way in which the rough and the smooth are the same:

The landscape was clothed in a mild and quiet light, in which the woods and fences checkered and partitioned it with new regularity, and rough and uneven fields stretched away with lawnlike smoothness to the horizon, and the clouds, finely distinct and picturesque, seemed to fit a drapery to hang over fairy-land.

Thus all our preferences, from the weakest down to the strongest, must be seen as one-sided, not in the sense that there are other justifiable points of view, but that the thing is simply *not* what we suppose it to be, the quality ascribed to it is entirely absent. Then what is the thing if it is devoid of all qualities? It is devoid of the absence of those qualities, and what is meant by this unpalatable conglomeration of negatives is that in some mysterious way the thing is alive, it exists with a palpitating stillness. A dark, invisible radiance comes from it, it moves from nowhere to nowhere, its future and its past ever present. It is the Way it travels; however small it fills all space; it is the Ground of Being and the Flowers of the Spirit that spring from it. It is the intimations of immortality and the certainty of annihilation.

THE ACTIVITY OF THE GREAT WAY IS VAST; IT IS NEITHER EASY NOR DIFFICULT.

The Way is called Great because there is nowhere else to walk but on it:

There is nothing difficult or easy about it, for it includes all existence and all nonexistence, all that is and all that can never be. We think it is easy and it is not; we suppose it to be difficult, and it is not. The ease or difficulty is entirely in our fancy. But this fancy also is included in the vastness of the activity of the Great Way and forms an essential part of it.

SMALL VIEWS ARE FULL OF FOXY FEARS; THE FASTER THE SLOWER.

Nothing can be achieved without courage. We fear to give up the bird in the hand for the two in the bush. This bird in the hand is not only life itself, but, for example, the Fatherhood of God. When we give up life, we pass beyond life and death. When we give up the Fatherhood of God, we lose also the feeling of dependence and servility. But we are still alive, God is still Our Father—but with a difference. Even with doubt there is the small view and the large view, the former an over-cautiousness, unadventurousness like that of the fox who will not venture on the ice until it is safe for an elephant; and the Great Doubt, which is the positive, active, thrusting doubt akin to curiosity but much stronger and deeper.

Ordinary study is cumulative, but with Zen it is not so, because it belongs to the timeless. This is why it is said, "The faster the slower." The more you search, the farther away it gets, for it is an open secret. To love God and love one's fellow man—there is nothing beyond this, nothing that requires explanation.

> **WHEN WE ATTACH OURSELVES TO THIS (IDEA OF ENLIGHTENMENT), WE LOSE OUR BALANCE: WE INFALLIBLY ENTER THE CROOKED WAY.**

Our experience, our deepest experience has taught us something; we wish to convey it to others. When they question its validity, we become angry, losing our mental serenity by holding so firmly to what is after all more intangible than snowflakes or the rainbow. It is not merely calmness of mind that we have lost, however, but what is this and more, the Middle Way, the knowledge (and practice) that our profoundest interpretation of life also must be thrown overboard together with the sentimentality, cruelty, snobbery, and folly that make our lives a misery. The Crooked Way is not a morally distorted manner of life. It is composed of virtues as much as of vices, of ideals, religious dogmas, principles of freedom and justice, as much as of degradation and tyranny. The Crooked Way is over-grieving at inevitable sorrows, over-clinging to joys which must cease; it is regarding as permanent what is but transitory; always looking for the silver lining, desiring to be in the nonexistent and impossible "Land beyond the morning star."

WHEN WE ARE NOT ATTACHED TO ANYTHING, ALL THINGS ARE AS THEY ARE: WITH ACTIVITY THERE IS NO GOING, NO STAYING.

Seize it and your hands are empty; drop it and they are full to overflowing. Ask, and ye shall not receive, is the iron law. But this non-asking is no indifference or blankness. It is like the "weakness" of women that overcomes the strongest man. It is like the force of gravity which pulls down the highest towers with not a single movement on its own part. Buds open in spring without straining; leaves fall in autumn without reluctance. The seasons come and go, years and centuries—but not the Activity, not the Great Way. There is no presence or absence, no increase or diminution with that.

OBEYING OUR NATURE, WE ARE IN ACCORD WITH THE WAY, WANDERING FREELY, WITHOUT ANNOYANCE.

Our own nature is not different from the nature of all things in which there is nothing unnatural. The fiends of Hell, the monsters of the deepest seas, the bacteria of our bosoms, the perversions of maniacs cannot surprise or disgust us. Living by Zen or without it, in perpetual fear and irritation; sadism and masochism; the destruction of life and beauty; the annihilation of the universe—none of these things can appall us. Our own faults and shortcomings, crimes and follies are a pleasure to us; the punishment they bring to us and to others is yet another confirmation of our insight into our true nature, overlaid as it is with illusions and superimposed habits that have become instincts, and usurp the authority of the Activity that yet works unceasingly within and without us.

WHEN OUR THINKING IS TIED, IT IS DARK, SUBMERGED, WRONG.

It is *dark*, so that we cannot distinguish the true nature of things; we see friends as enemies, strengthening trials as useless annoyances. We fail to perceive the so-called defects and errors of others as an aspect of their Buddha nature. It is *submerged*; it does not float upon the waves of circumstances that can both drown or buoy us up. When all things work together for good because we love God, that is, we seek not to change that which is inevitable, the outside, but only the free, the inside, then we are as light as corks however low the billows descend, however high they mount aloft. It is *wrong*, because our nature is freedom. Perfect service, no task left undone or scamped, as best exemplified in a mother's unfailing, tender care, is right because not tied by duty or public opinion.

IT IS FOOLISH TO IRRITATE YOUR MIND; WHY SHUN THIS AND BE FRIENDS WITH THAT?

Our ordinary mind, our ordinary life consists of nothing else but avoiding this and pursuing that, but the life of "reason," that rises up at times from some submerged realm into conscious life is far other:

> *The mind, when once it has withdrawn itself to itself and realized its own power, has neither part nor lot with the soft and pleasant, or harsh and painful motions of thy breath.*
>
> —Marcus Aurelius

IF YOU WISH TO TRAVEL IN THE VEHICLE, DO NOT DISLIKE THE SIX DUSTS.

The Six Dusts are the qualities produced by the objects and organs of sense: sight, sound, smell, taste, touch, and idea. The One Vehicle is the Mahayana, the vehicle of Oneness. The *Saddharmapundarika Sutra (Hokkekyo)* says:

> *Only one vehicle of the Law,*
> *Not two, and not three.*

The Six Dusts, that is, the body and its attendant misguided ideas, are the cause of all our unhappiness and suffering, and prevent us from seeing things as they really are and from having the peace of mind that is our birthright. But an old waka says, illustrating the way in which nothing is good or bad of its nature, but thinking makes it so:

> *Sin and evil*
> *Are not to be got rid of*
> *Just blindly;*
> *Look at the astringent persimmons!*
> *They turn into the sweet dried ones.*

INDEED, NOT HATING THE SIX DUSTS IS IDENTICAL WITH REAL ENLIGHTENMENT.

This absence of hatred, of intolerance, disgust, righteous indignation, discrimination and judging, is itself the state of Buddhahood. This negativeness, however, is not that of the opposite of affirmation. It is not the passive condition it seems to be, neither can it be described by the words "love your enemies." It is not absence of feeling, or indifference, but some unnameable attitude of mind in which evil is accepted as such, though not condoned. It is described by George Eliot in the following way:

> *"Ay sir," said Luke, as he gave his arm to his master, "you'll make up your mind to it a bit better, when you've seen everything; you'll get used to it. That's what my mother says about her shortness of breath—she says she's made friends wi' it, though she fought against it when it first came on."*

In a word, we must not hate hatred.

**THE WISE MAN DOES NOTHING,
THE FOOL SHACKLES HIMSELF.**

This "wise passivity" is that of nature:

*The buds swell imperceptibly without hurry or
confusion, as if the short spring day were an
eternity.*

—Thoreau

We bind ourselves with our likes and dislikes, we
are bound with fancied bonds. There is nothing so
strong in the world as a delusion, nothing so indestructible as this imaginary, nonexistent self and
its temporary profit and loss, loving and loathing.

**THE TRUTH HAS NO DISTINCTIONS; THESE
COME FROM OUR FOOLISH CLINGING
TO THIS AND THAT.**

There is the distinction between the wise man
and the fool, a wise thought and a foolish one, but
none in the Nature of Things. Here there is perfect uniformity, law, and equality. Mountains and
rivers, birds, beasts, and flowers are all one undivided indivisible thing. Yet on the other hand, each
thing is itself and no other thing, unique, irre-
placeable, and invaluable. Sameness and difference

are also one thing, yet two things. At one moment we see the separate meaning of a thing, at another, its meaning as being all things; and at some most precious moments of all, incommunicable in speech but yet heard also through it, we know that a thing, a person, a flower, the cry of a bird, is both one thing and all things. Sameness and difference, and *their* sameness and difference are the same and yet different from our own nonexistence.

SEEKING THE MIND WITH THE MIND—IS NOT THIS THE GREATEST OF ALL MISTAKES?

Clinging to the search for the mind is the last infirmity of the religious soul, and the most self-evidently absurd, for why should we search for the Buddha that we have already, why seek to release ourselves from bonds that are only fancied? But it is the greediness of our searching which invalidates it. This is beautifully expressed in the following:

There is a treasure in the deep mountains;
He who has no desire for it finds it.

ILLUSION PRODUCES REST AND MOTION; ILLUMINATION DESTROYS LIKING AND DISLIKING.

The state of the ordinary man is one in which he is continually either peacefully contented by successful activity, or in the anxious throes of that activity, either winning or losing, having won or having lost. The enlightened man loses well and wins well.

ALL THESE PAIRS OF OPPOSITES ARE CREATED BY OUR OWN FOLLY.

Once Dogen was approached by a short-tempered man and asked to cure his short-temperedness. Dogen asked him to show his shortness of temper, but the man confessed his inability to do so. It had no real existence, any more than his patience. Both are created by our own folly and idle fancy. When our minds are full of something, not part of a thing, but all of it, when there is no vacancy for odds and ends of passion to occupy, we act without rashness or hesitation. What the Third Patriarch says is very much akin to the old proverb, "Satan finds some mischief still for idle hands to do."

DREAMS, DELUSIONS, FLOWERS OF AIR—WHY SHOULD WE BE SO ANXIOUS TO HAVE THEM IN OUR GRASP?

These creations of the mind, so common and habitual that there seems to be some concrete reality behind them, are the protagonists of all tragic drama. Fixed notions of honor, propriety, faithfulness, conflict of necessity with the imperturbable, ineffable, and intangible truth that ultimately destroys them. Rigidity versus fluidity, the name versus the nameless; yet in this very willingness to die for some impossible creed we see once more that just as the ordinary man, as he is, is the Buddha, so these delusions are, as they stand, the truth, and without them there is no reality. What is wrong is the anxiety to reject them. Error or truth, profit or loss—if we accept them readily, cheerfully, as in some sense ministers of God, remembering that even the devils fear and serve Him, these flowers of the air also have their beauty and value.

PROFIT AND LOSS, RIGHT AND WRONG— AWAY WITH THEM ONCE FOR ALL!

What Sengtsan means here, is that we are to give up the false idea that profit actually profits us, that there is any individual self to suffer loss or gain. Forgetting all moral principles, we are to *"Dilige et quod vis fac."* (Love, and do as you please.) This abstention from choosing, from judging, does not mean that we do not choose as pleasant or judge as wrong. What it means is that God does it for us, God who is so often disobeyed, who turns the other cheek and forgives his enemies. When, for example, we give an order, as a teacher, or an official, it is to be given peremptorily without a thought of the possibility of its not being obeyed. But if it is not obeyed, there is no *personal* irritation and wounded vanity in the angry remonstrance we make. A law of nature, of human society has been broken, and it is right that our emotion should be aroused by this.

The doctrine that in all our acts we are to be vice-gerents of Nature is a dangerous one, but every truth is dangerous, for it liberates universal energies that may easily go astray. Religious persecution, megalomania, political fanaticism are all misuses of what the Third Patriarch inculcates. But we know them by their fruits; by the defects, the distortions, the hatreds of the dictators.

IF THE EYE DOES NOT SLEEP, ALL DREAMING CEASES NATURALLY.

Human life is a dream, not in its brevity and discontinuity, but in the fact that we see things almost always as related to our own personal interests. But we must "persist in our folly" to the bitter end, and say,

My God, my God, why hast thou forsaken me?

At such moments we wake and see things as they really are, in their suchness, the nails in the wood, the wood in the ground, the sun setting in the western sky, a mother weeping for her son, a manless, Godless universe, each thing fulfilling the law of its being. When we wake from our sleep of relativity and subjectivism, nightmares of glory and disgrace, flattery and condemnation will cease of themselves.

IF THE MIND MAKES NO DISCRIMINATIONS, ALL THINGS ARE AS THEY REALLY ARE.

Things are all right, if only we will let them be alone, cooperate with them, take lead as heavy and use it as a plummet, take swords as sharp and receive the surgeon's knife, take pain as dreadful but not as something distinct from ourselves, adding imagination to reality. Yungchia describes this condition in the following way:

The moon reflected in the stream, the wind blowing through the pines
In the cool of the evening, in the deep midnight—
what is it for?

It is all for nothing, for itself, for others. This is the suchness of things.

IN THE DEEP MYSTERY OF THIS "THINGS AS THEY ARE," WE ARE RELEASED FROM OUR RELATIONS TO THEM.

Things as they are, the coldness of ice and the sound of rain, the fall of leaves and the silence of the sky, are ultimate things, never to be questioned, never to be explained away. When we know them, our relations to them, their use and misuses, their associated pleasures and pains are all forgotten.

WHEN ALL THINGS ARE SEEN "WITH EQUAL MIND," THEY RETURN TO THEIR NATURE.

This "equal mind" of Matthew Arnold is that which speaks in the words of Marcus Aurelius:

All that happens is as usual and familiar as the rose in spring and the crop in summer.

NO DESCRIPTION BY ANALOGY IS POSSIBLE OF THIS STATE WHERE ALL RELATIONS HAVE CEASED.

Metaphors and similes, parables and comparisons may be used to describe anything belonging to the relative, the intellectually dichotomized world, but even the simplest and commonest experience of reality, the touch of hot water, the smell of camphor, are incommunicable by such or any means; how much more so the Fatherhood of God, the Meaningless of Meaning, the Absolute Value of a popcorn, for in such matters, the unity of our own emptiness and that of all other things is perceived as an act of self-consciousness, and nothing remains to be compared with anything. In Chapter VII of the *Platform Sutra* we are told of Nanyueh, 677–744, and his meeting with Huineng, the Sixth Patriarch, who asked him from whence he had come. "From Suzan," he replied. "What comes? How did it come?" asked the Patriarch.

Nanyueh replied, "We cannot say it is similar to anything."

WHEN WE STOP MOVEMENT, THERE IS NO-MOVEMENT; WHEN WE STOP RESTING, THERE IS NO-REST.

Neither rest nor movement has any reality as such; they are two names of one thinglessness which cannot be caused to cease, because it is uncreated. There is a waka which says:

> *When it blows,*
> *How noisy*
> *The mountain wind!*
> *But when it blows not,*
> *Where will it have gone?*

Blowing, not blowing, what is there but nothingness, an invisible, intangible something-heard-and-not-heard?

WHEN BOTH CEASE TO BE, HOW CAN THE UNITY SUBSIST?

There is no more a unity than there is duality; relative and absolute are names of the nameless. Zen, that is to say, is a word that is used like an algebraic sign, for all that is nameless, all that escapes thought, definition, explanation, yet breathes through words and silence; is communicated in spite of our best efforts to communicate it. Actions are either good or bad; yet nothing is good or bad, but thinking makes it so. That is to say, things are both good or bad and neither; relative and absolute; or, if you wish it, neither relative nor absolute, there is neither duality nor a unity.

THINGS ARE ULTIMATELY, IN THEIR FINALITY, SUBJECT TO NO LAW.

"No law" means no scientific, psychological, logical, philosophical, Buddhist, or any other kind of law. As D. H. Lawrence says, "Life is what one wants in one's soul." It is not something imposed upon us from without. Law is indeed an intellectual, rational conception, and applies only to the intellectual, rational aspect of things abstracted from the whole.

FOR THE ACCORDANT MIND IN ITS UNITY, INDIVIDUAL ACTIVITY CEASES.

When the mind is in accord with all creatures and with the Buddha, one with all things, its activity as an individual entity ceases. What Mozart was at the piano, Bach at the organ, Shakespeare with his pen, Turner with his brush, we are with our most trivial and personal affairs of life. When this is not so, when our acts are hesitant, our work repugnant, our life full of fears for the morrow and regret for the past, even the spider in its web, the violet by the stone give us that feeling of envy, a realization of our alienation from God that no pleasure can assuage.

ALL DOUBTS ARE CLEARED UP, TRUE FAITH IS CONFIRMED.

Doubt and faith are concerned with one thing and one thing only, the Goodness of the universe. And this is tested by us most intimately and searchingly within ourselves. If at the outset we stipulate a personal Deity, individual immortality and so on, no resolution of doubt and establishment of faith are possible. We are to make no demands whatever upon the world. "Judge not" is the word here too. Standing apart from things and questioning them, praising and condemning—this is the cardinal error. Living their life, dying their death, being cloven with the worm and shriveled in the candle flame with the moth, is the only way to solve the mystery of fruitless suffering, the problem of the waste of beauty and goodness.

NOTHING REMAINS BEHIND; THERE IS NOT ANYTHING WE MUST REMEMBER.

We are not bound by any "imitation of Buddha." There are no snags, no undigested material, no fitting in with preconceived notions, no formulae to follow in the way of our life or manner of death. We may be confirmed or baptized if we feel it is good for us, or die at the stake rather than submit to it. And we extend the same privilege to everyone else. No one need be converted to this or that religion. When we do wrong or make mistakes, we go on with renewed vigor to the next task; a faux pas cannot check us or make us dwell on it with self-torturing shame.

EMPTY, LUCID, SELF-ILLUMINATED, WITH NO OVER-EXERTION OF THE POWER OF THE MIND.

Empty means with nothing clogging the mind, no trace of self-interest. Lucid means seeing unreason as clearly as reason, reflecting ugliness as serenely as beauty. Self-illuminated means truth is not revealed to it from some outside agency.

Over-exertion of the power of the mind is that of Othello, Mr. Tulliver, Mr. Dombey, and the protagonists of all tragic drama. There is nothing tragic or comic, but thinking makes it so, the thinking of the actors and the sympathetic thinking of the self-illuminated spectators, who see their self-interest and grieve for it, perceive the self-defacement and unreasonableness without the reflecting surface of their own minds being marred by it.

THIS IS WHERE THOUGHT IS USELESS,
WHAT KNOWLEDGE CANNOT FATHOM.

This verse looks back to a passage in the *Lotus Sutra:*

This law cannot be known properly by thought and discrimination,

and looks forward to the reply of Yunmen to a certain monk who asked, "What is this place where thought is useless?", "Knowledge and emotion cannot fathom it!" To express this thoughtless, knowledgeless, emotionless state, in which thought and knowledge and emotion are sublimed into instinct of the highest order, we have such a phrase as,

The lotus blooms in the midst of the fire.

But this is too intellectual in its denial and rejection of the intellect. Better is the following, from Thoreau:

The weeds at the bottom gently bending down the stream, shaken by the watery wind, still planted where their seeds had sunk, but ere long to die and go down likewise; the shining pebbles, not yet anxious to better their condition; the chips and reeds, and occasional logs and stems of trees that floated past, fulfilling their fate, were objects of singular interest to me, and at last I resolved to launch myself on its bosom and float whither it would bear me.

IN THE WORLD OF REALITY, THERE IS NO SELF, NO OTHER THAN SELF.

To say this is easy, to believe it intellectually is not difficult. It has an emotional, a poetical appeal which few can withstand. With a full belly, a bank balance, when all is going well, such a doctrine will be readily adopted. But when food is scarce, when a man has lost his job, in hours of boredom, when children die, and our own death is not far off—can we then rejoice with those that rejoice and mourn with those that mourn? In my own case, I must say that nothing makes me more contented with my lot than to see the sufferings of others, to find my children cleverer and prettier than those of my colleagues. How far indeed is this from the lines above.

SHOULD YOU DESIRE IMMEDIATE CORRESPONDENCE (WITH THIS REALITY), ALL THAT CAN BE SAID IS, "NO DUALITY!"

But even this "No duality," no relativity, no choosing, no judging, is not to be elevated into a principle of living. It may be used as a touchstone of past conduct, or as an ideal for some possible future situation, but for living, which is the eternal present only, all that can be said is nothing whatever.

WHEN THERE IS NO DUALITY, ALL THINGS ARE ONE. THERE IS NOTHING THAT IS NOT INCLUDED.

When Thoreau lay dying, he was asked if he had made his peace with God; he answered, "We have never quarreled." In Thoreau's world, everything was included, nothing rejected and made into an enemy. Where there is no duality there can be no quarreling. When God lived for two years by Walden lake, Thoreau did not criticize, praise, or condemn Him. As St. Augustine says,

> *To live happily is to live according to the mind of God.*

THE ENLIGHTENED OF ALL TIMES AND PLACES HAVE EVERY ONE ENTERED INTO THIS TRUTH.

This sounds rather depressing, as though ordinary people were excluded, but what Sengtsan means is that comparatively few know that they have entered into the realm of Buddhahood, where all men and all things without exception have their (unconscious and unwitting) being. Not a sparrow can fall out of God's care, nor can anyone, for all his hair shirts and flagellations enter into His providence. It is only a question of becoming aware of our true condition, and this becoming aware is called "entering."

**TRUTH CANNOT BE INCREASED OR DECREASED;
AN INSTANTANEOUS THOUGHT LASTS A
MYRIAD YEARS.**

The bonds of time and space do not prevail against the Truth, the Way, the Buddha Mind. Long and short, here and there, a moment and eternity are all included in it, as names alone. Blake says,

One thought fills immensity.

**THERE IS NO HERE, NO THERE,
INFINITY IS BEFORE OUR EYES.**

Here and there are dualities and therefore obstructions to the life of perfection. Infinity is under our noses, our noses are infinitely long. Yungchia says,

*The Mirror of the Mind brightly shining,
    unobstructed,
Passes transparently through everything in
    the universe.*

When this Mind is our mind, when we are not bored with here and longing to be there, when the life of things is breathed in and breathed out with every breath we take, when we live in the past of our world and into the unborn future without desiring to undo what is done, or avoid what must be, then we live a timeless life now, a placeless life here.

THE INFINITELY SMALL IS AS LARGE AS THE INFINITELY GREAT, FOR LIMITS ARE NONEXISTENT THINGS.

This is a kind of *reductio ad absurdum* of the unpoetic, common-sense position, that great and small are mutually exclusive qualities. If the extremes meet, so does the middle and all the rest. Limits and boundaries are man-made things, and what man has put together, man can put asunder. A doka which illustrates this is the following:

> *Mount Fuji*
> *Good in fine weather,*
> *Good in the rain:*
> *The Original Form*
> *Never changes.*

THE INFINITELY LARGE IS AS SMALL AS THE INFINITELY MINUTE; NO EYE CAN SEE THEIR BOUNDARIES.

Lying at night in camp, Thoreau speaks of

> *The barking of the house dogs, from the loudest and hoarsest bark to the faintest aerial palpitation under the eaves of heaven.*

There is the most extreme form of expression of the Mahayana theory that corresponds to the Christian doctrine (mystical and, strictly speaking, heretical) that God is above all qualities, all predications, even of existence. The "is-ness" of things is a fantasy of life's fitful fever—but so is their "is-not-ness." Life is a dream, but so is this statement. This last fact is hard to catch. When we say that unreality is also unreal, in our normal moments, and especially when the mind is tired, this means nothing, or less than nothing. It irritates by its illogicality, and is repugnant because of the demand it makes that we are unable to supply. It is therefore necessary that we say such things, to ourselves or others, only when we are in a condition of mind to know what we are saying, otherwise by frequent vain repetitions we shall become as the heathen, unable to recognize moments of vision when they visit us. So for example, death is a fearful thing because of its irrevocableness, but at times, when perhaps least expected, or even unwanted, the realization comes to us that what has never existed, the individual soul, the ego, has not gone and cannot go out of existence. What was born, immediately ceased to be. At every moment, neither existence nor nonexistence can be predicated or denied—yet what a world of difference between a living child and a dead one!

Consider the following sentence of Thoreau's, put into the form of a haiku:

Over the old wooden bridge
No traveler
Crossed.

This no-traveler, like deserted roads, empty chairs, silent organs, has more meaning, more poetry, solidity and permanence than any traveler. "No traveler" does not mean nobody, nothing at all; it means every-man, you and I and God and all things cross this old rickety bridge, and like the bold lover on the Grecian Urn can never reach the goal.

UNTIL YOU HAVE GRASPED THIS FACT, YOUR POSITION IS SIMPLY UNTENABLE.

Common sense is revolted by the above assertion that what is, is not, what is not, is, but in actual practice it is found to be the only valid one. The story of the monk who was praised for bringing a basket to catch the drips from a leaking roof illustrated this identity of what is and what is not. A bucket or a basket, there is no difference. One man's meat is another man's poison. A leaf of grass is a six-foot golden Buddha. Life is a perpetual dying. And if you keep to the so-called commonsense point of view (which is more elastic than supposed), you will find that your hard-and-fast divisions between right and wrong, profit and loss, useful and harmful, are inapplicable to all your problems and indeed to every circumstance of life that is deeply felt and profoundly experienced.

ONE THING IS ALL THINGS;
ALL THINGS ARE ONE THING.

This expresses in an extreme form the state of Mind toward which things are constantly tending, called paradox by logic, metaphor by literature, genius or madness by popular consent. The humorist says, describing the beauty of a certain film actress, "When she comes into the room, the room comes in with her," and forget it, but another step has been taken toward the region where

One sentence decides heaven and earth;
One sword pacifies all sublunary things.

When you have really seen one flower, you have seen not only all flowers, but all non-flowers. One principle, one life, one animate or inanimate manifestation moves and upholds all things.

IF THIS IS SO FOR YOU, THERE IS NO NEED TO WORRY ABOUT PERFECT KNOWLEDGE.

Worry is the great enemy. The search for enlightenment obscures and delays it. What is wrong is not the pain and grief of suffering, but thinking about ourselves as sufferers. As Mussolini said, "Never look back." Therefore, when, if only temporarily, we see into the unity of the life of the multifarious things of this world, do not let us lose our firm conviction of this vision by thoughts of our sins of omission and commission, inconsistency of words and actions. Thoreau says of the cry of the cock:

> The merit of this bird's strain is in its freedom from all plaintiveness. The singer can easily move us to tears or laughter, but where is he who can excite in us a pure morning joy. When, in doleful dumps, breaking the awful stillness of our wooden sidewalk on a Sunday, or, perchance, a watcher in the house of mourning, I hear a cockerel crow far or near, I think to myself, "There is one of us well, at any rate,"—and with a sudden rush return to my senses.

It is the same spirit that breathes in the words of Miyamoto Musashi, great swordsman and painter:

> As far as I am concerned, I regret nothing.

THE BELIEVING MIND IS NOT DUAL; WHAT IS DUAL IS NOT THE BELIEVING MIND.

When we believe in *something*, this is not the believing mind. If we say we believe in ourselves, this again is a mistake, of experience or of expression. "The believing mind believes in itself"—this, rightly understood, contains no error. The *Lankavatara Sutra* says,

> Believing in the truth of timeless life is called the Believing Mind.

Clearer still is the *Nirvana Sutra:*

The Believing Mind is the Buddha nature.

Here there is no danger of one thing believing in another thing. The Buddha nature is the true nature of every thing and of everything. The believing mind is this Buddha activity. A Haydn minuet or the Lord's prayer or a kitten catching at the falling autumn leaves is a clear thought of this mind, a harmonious movement of the Buddha nature. It is perfect because it is single, unique, complete, all-including.

BEYOND ALL LANGUAGE; FOR IT, THERE IS NO PAST, NO PRESENT, NO FUTURE.

Language is vitally concerned with time, with tense. The Way is timeless and breaks through language, but does not discard it. Silence itself is a form of speaking, just as the blank spaces between the marks of the printing are as much part of the printing as the letters themselves. The Way is timeless yet it cannot dispense with time. Eternity and time are in love with each other, continually embracing in a divine union, yet always separate to the purely human eye.

2. PLOYS AND MANEUVERS

**Famous mondoes
of the great Zen masters**

1. BUNS

A monk asked Ummon, "What is it that surpasses the Buddhas, surpasses the Patriarchs?" Ummon replied, "Buns."

The Buddhas and the Patriarchs are things of the mind, just like generals and prime ministers and policemen, but buns are real, buns are earnest; they have a simplicity, a perfection of being which no man can attain to. Jesus taught us to pray for our daily buns. They are also the spiritual Body of Christ, broken for us. Above all, buns are something which Buddhas and gods and sages are not (except unintentionally); they are humorous.

2. THE WORDLESS WORD

A monk asked Roso, "What is the wordless word?" Roso said, "Where's your mouth?" The monk said,

*"I haven't got one!" "What do you eat with then?"
asked Roso. The monk had no reply.*

The point of this lies in Roso's question,
"Where is your mouth?" If it is in the (relative)
face, it must be either wordful or wordless. If it is
in the (absolute) spiritual body, it is neither wordful nor wordless. What we need is the mouth that
utters wordless words (and wordful silence).

3. I DON'T BOW

*Rinzai visited the stupa at Yuji (where Daruma
was supposed to have been buried). The keeper
asked Rinzai, "Do you bow to the Buddha first, or
to Daruma first?" Rinzai replied, "I don't bow to
either of them." The keeper asked, "Why are you
and the Buddha and Daruma enemies?" Rinzai
shook his sleeves and went away.*

When Rinzai says he doesn't bow to either, he
does not mean that he does not bow to one more
than the other. He means that he does not bow to
either. He does not bow to the universe, or to the
Truth. He does not bow even to Bach or Basho.
He does not bow at all, any more than the universe bows to him. The keeper of the stupa was
suitable to his job in a way; he was stupid.

4. HELP ME UP!

One day Joshu fell down in the snow, and called out, "Help me up! Help me up!" A monk came and lay down beside him. Joshu got up and went away.

We cannot help other people, in things that really matter. We can only look or act our fellow-feeling. Christ cannot take us to heaven. We have to go with our own wings. This is not mere *jiriki*, self-power, but a condition where *tariki*, other-power, and *jiriki* are one and the same thing, so strictly speaking we cannot say that Christ does not "lift us up" or that we lift ourselves up by our own faith. We can only go up, or not. But—and this is the point of the anecdote—we must show our awareness of the rising or not rising of others. That is our humanity.

5. MOO!

One day Ummon asked, "How can we make our religion proper?" Answering himself, he said, "Moo!"

This has perhaps two meanings: first, we can't; second, we can, but only by purely animal methods. A cow strengthens its lungs, and advertises its cowness by mooing. It moos itself into being a cow. No moo, no cow; no cow, no moo, so the children rightly call it a moo-cow. Zen must be the same.

6. A RIDDLE

Hyakujo said to his monks, "There's a man who eats sparingly, but is never hungry; there's a man who is always eating, and never full." The monks had nothing to say.

We must be both these men, always overflowing with energy, but never ambitious. By not going we arrive. Fully satisfied at each moment, we never remain with it. Whether Hyakujo meant this is not the question. When a master of (his own) Zen speaks, I must respond with (my own) Zen, if any.

7. TAP-TAP

Nansen's cook-monk invited the gardener-monk to have a meal together, and went to his house and was waiting for him. As he filled his bowl, a Nembutsu Bird sang. The gardener-monk tapped his arm-rest, and the bird sang again. He tapped the arm-rest again and the bird stopped singing. The gardener-monk asked, "Do you understand?" "No," said the cook-monk. The gardener-monk tapped once more.

This is a strange story, as if out of Andersen's Fairy Tales, but evidently the point is the gardener-monk's rapport with Nature and the cook-monk's lack of it. In the last tapping, the gardener-monk is making a bit of music on his own, but the cook-monk has no ears to hear.

8. KNOCK AT THE DOOR

A monk knocked at Bokushu's door, saying, "Clear me up! I ask you to direct me!" Bokushu said, "I have a stick here for you!" The monk had hardly opened the door and began to ask something when Bokushu immediately struck him.

What the monk can learn from this, what Bokushu wants to teach him, is that when we do something, we are done by something. This doing and being done to is life, and when conscious willingness is added to do and done to, there is Zen. We therefore revise Christ's words, "Knock, and it shall be opened unto you," to, "Knock, and ye shall be knocked."

9. QUITE!

A monk said to Ummon, "If a man kills his father, kills his mother, he may repent before the Buddha. If he kills the Buddha, kills a patriarch, where can he repent?" Ummon answered, "Quite!"

This is an example of the one-syllable replies for which Ummon is justly famous. *Ro! (Lu!)* means "expressed," "clear," "nothing hidden," and corresponds very well to the English idiomatic use of "Quite!" What Ummon means is that the question is a very good one, that is, it is rhetorical. Such a man has no place to repent, nowhere to repent; he can't repent. What we can't do, we shouldn't do. As Thoreau says, "Nature never apologizes." Dogs fawn, like men, but a cat just licks itself in the corner when slapped.

10. RICE IN THE POT

A monk asked Kankei, "What is the meaning of Daruma's coming from the West?" He answered, "Rice in the bowl, stew in the pot." The monk said, "I don't understand." Kankei said, "Eating while you're hungry, stopping when you're full."

Saying this kind of thing without at least hinting at its relation with the question must be called the tender mercies of the wicked. If Kankei had said, "Zen is doing completely and wholeheartedly whatever you are doing," the monk might have got something, and then if he had continued, "Making mistakes and being afraid with all your heart and mind and soul," the monk would not have been enlightened, but he would at least have been disillusioned, and the only other alternative would be to strike him. "A smoking flax shalt thou not quench" but we may jump on a fire and put it out.

11. BAMBOO SHOOTS

Joshu asked an old woman with a basket, "Where are you off to?" "I am going to steal your bamboo shoots," she replied. Joshu said, "Suppose you meet me soon after, what then?" The old woman gave him a slap on the face. Joshu gave up and went away.

Some of these old Chinese women were more than a match for the greatest Zen masters. By saying she would steal his bamboo sprouts, she meant perhaps his special ways of teaching and so on. Joshu asks her if she would not be ashamed of doing such a thing, and she immediately strikes him, showing her beyond-good-and-evil mind.

12. RHINOCEROS FAN

Enkan, dates unknown, a disciple of Baso, is known for the anecdote of the Rhinoceros Fan. He told a monk to fetch his fan. The monk said, "It is broken." "If it's broken, then give me the rhinoceros," said Enkan. The monk made no reply.

By saying, "It is broken," the monk meant that the fan was "empty" of real being. Enkan agreed, then asked the monk to show the reality of things, but the monk could not. He understood that "All things are devoid of self nature," but not that "All abstractions are concrete." At this time Shifuku (Tzufu) was present; he drew in the air a circle, and within it the character for cow, which forms part of the character for rhinoceros. By so doing he acted the fact that "All concrete things are abstract," and that "Transcendentals are material."

13. FROM KOZEI

Seppo asked a monk where he had come from. "From Kozei," said the monk. "Did you meet Daruma anywhere?" asked Seppo. "I just left him," replied the monk.

This anecdote is a refreshing change from the usual reduction of the monk to a half-imbecile silence. The monk has learned to play the Zen game, and airily displays his virtuosity. Though not very profound, it is perhaps superior to Ping-Pong and such sports.

14. I'D BE DUMBFOUNDED

A monk of Kassan's went to Kotei and had just bowed to him when Kotei struck him on the back. The monk bowed again, and again Kotei struck him, and drove him away. The monk told Kassan about this, and Kassan asked, "Do you understand?" "No," replied the monk. "That's a good thing," said Kassan, "for if you did, I would be dumbfounded."

Nyogen Senzaki has a fine comment on this anecdote. "American Zen is running sideways, writing books, lecturing, referring to theology, psychology, and what not. Someone should stand up and smash the whole thing to pieces. . . ."

15. NO UNDERSTANDING

A monk said to Eimyo, "I have been with you a long time, but I have yet to grasp your way of looking at things." Eimyo said, "Understand that you don't understand!" The monk said, "If I don't understand, how can I understand anything?" Eimyo replied, "The womb of a cow gives birth to an elephant, and the blue sea produces yellow dust."

Eimyo's intention is clearly to make the understanding monk understand less. When we feel an exhilaration in the non-understanding we are close to Zen.

16. SUPREME TEACHING

Seppo first visited Enkan, then Tosu, three times, and Tozan nine times, without results, and at last asked Tokusan, "Is it possible for me too to share,

with the patriarchs, in the Supreme Teaching?"
Tokusan struck him with his staff, saying, "What
on earth are you talking about?" The next day he
asked for an explanation. Tokusan said, "My reli-
gion has no words and sentences; it has nothing to
give anybody." At this Seppo became enlightened.

Tokusan says that Zen is wordless, and that it is
not something. Zen may be words. All living, poetical words are Zen. Zen is not, however, the meaning of the words. It is the words themselves, with
their meaning not perceived separately from the
words. Zen also is not something which can be
given or received. Love is the same. We can't give
love to God; God can't give it to us. God *is* love.
When we really know, with our body-mind, that
there is nothing we can get or bestow, borrow or
lend, hold or lose, that we can't forgive or be for-
given, save or be saved (think of *The Man Who
Died*), we know Zen, but we don't know what it is,
because it isn't a what.

17. EATING CAKES

Gensha was one day eating cakes with General I
(Wei). The general said, "What is that which we
use every day, but don't know it?" Gensha picked
up a cake and said, "Have one!" The general took
it and ate it, and then repeated his question. Gen-
sha said, "We use it every day, but we don't know
it."

Gensha answers the real question, which is asked by the general's stomach, bowels of cleverness. The Jewish answer was, "Underneath are the everlasting arms," but people then gabble about anthropomorphism, or worse still about comparative religion. One great advantage of the Zen bun-eating answer to all theological questions is that you can hardly go to war about it. Perhaps this is the Zen way of abolishing war, the generals, and, still more dangerous, the privates!

18. NO IDEA

A monk asked Ummon, "What are the activities of a Sramana?" Ummon answered, "I have not the slightest idea." The monk then said, "Why haven't you any idea?" Ummon replied, "I just want to keep my no-idea."

A sramana is a monk, an enlightened monk. The Sanskrit root of the word is *sram*, to make efforts, to do austerities. This monk's question is not so much "What shall I do to be saved?" as "What does a man do when he is saved?" Ummon's answer may be interpreted in many ways. "I know, but I don't want to say." "I really don't know." "I want to teach you not to know." "My state of mind is beyond knowing and not knowing." "You are pestering me!" "Perfect action is unconscious of itself." "Don't ask (foolish) questions!" All these to some extent enter into his wish not to fall into the deadness of knowing something. After we are enlightened, what shall we do?

19. BOWING AND RISING

A monk came to be taught, and Isan, seeing him, made as if to rise. The monk said, "Please don't get up!" Isan said, "I haven't sat down yet!" The monk said, "I haven't bowed yet." Isan said, "You rude creature!"

We may suppose that the monk had already bowed, at least at the entrance of the room, and that when he said, "I haven't bowed yet," he was playing Isan's game of the absolute, but Isan suddenly jumps to the relative, and scolds the monk. As said before, we must always be in the absolute-relative (relative-absolute) and then we cannot be attacked from either relative or the absolute.

20. EARTHWORM

Shiko was one day hoeing a field and cut an earthworm into two. He said, "Today I have cut into two an earthworm. Both ends are moving; in which of them is the life?" He lifted up his hoe, hit each end of the worm with it, then the space between them, lifted up the hoe, and went back.

We divide life into two, good and bad, right and wrong, beautiful and ugly, desirable and undesirable, this and that. Can all the king's horses and all the king's men put Humpty Dumpty together again? This is what Shiko does, by admitting the division of the worm into two—almost into three—with the one hoe. The hoe that divides reunites the parts again. The hoe is the creative imagination, the one Buddha eye.

21. FLOWERS DON'T RETURN

A monk asked Kegon, "How about when an en-lightened man returns to illusion?" Kegon said, "A broken mirror does not reflect; fallen flowers do not go back to the branch."

This does not mean that an enlightened man is infallible and cannot make mistakes or do bad or foolish things. It means that he partakes of the inevitability of things. Just as the flowers make no effort to return to the branch or the broken mirror to be whole again, so the enlightened man does what he does without regret or self-pity.

22. SILLY OLD WOMAN

Mayoku and Nansen and another monk were on a Nature pilgrimage, intending to interview Kinzan, and met an old woman on the way. "Where do you live?" they asked. "Here," she said. The three went into her teashop. The old woman made a pot of tea, and brought three cups and put them on the table and said, "Let the one who has godlike power drink the tea!" The three looked at each other but nobody said anything, and nobody drank the tea. The old woman said, "This silly old woman will show you her full power. Just watch!" and she took the tea, drank it up, and departed.

The interesting thing is that as Bernard Shaw said, no woman is interesting until she is forty. When some (Chinese) women become quite old, they seem to get some occult power and become witches, or, as here, natural Zen adepts.

23. AN EXAMINATION

One day Chinso was up in a tower with other officials, and one of them, seeing a number of monks passing, said, "Those people coming are monks on pilgrimage." Chinso said, "It is not so." The other expostulated, "How can you say (know) that it is not so?" Chinso said, "Wait till they get near, and I will examine them." The monks came before the tower. Chinso called out to them, "Reverend gentlemen!" They all raised their heads and looked in his direction. "What did I tell you?" said Chinso.

I take the story like this. Chinso looks out of the window at the official's remark, and sees a group of monks approaching, and from their manner of walking, even in the distance, realizes that they are far from enlightened. He examines them by calling out to them in a polite way. Real monks would take no notice, but they all look up with foolish faces that bespeak the vacant mind. Even the official can see that they are without inner power and self-reliance. Enlightenment is invariably accompanied by the power to know who is enlightened and who is not, just as a love of animals (which is a form of enlightenment) enables us to distinguish the real and the sham love of animals in others.

24. SHALLOW OR DEEP?

A monk said to Ummon, "How about a man whose parents won't let him be a priest?" "Shallow!" said Ummon. "I am not uneducated, but I don't understand." "Deep!" said Ummon.

When we teach, we teach ourselves. If the student also understands something, that's fine, but it is unlikely. "Shallow" means the question is shallow, and the man who will not "Hate father and mother for my sake" is shallow. "Deep" means that to be troubled about a question is deep; not to know is (potentially) deep.

25. A SINGLE CLOUD

A monk asked Shozan, "Is there a sentence which does not belong to the realm of right and wrong, to is and is not?" Shozan said, "There is." "What is it?" asked the monk. "A single cloud floating in the sky has nothing ugly about it."

To say something which is logically neither affirmative nor negative is hardly possible, except for exclamations like *"Kwatz!"* or blows. Shozan indeed uses a kind of double alternative, in denying one of the pairs, ugly-beautiful. The point is that the sentence, which is not dichotomous, is so because of the person who says it, the way he says it, his state of mind before and after saying it. Thus Shozan's sentence is Shozan's; we can hardly repeat it as an example of absoluteness, for it becomes repetitious, artificial, and calculated. We must have Iago's motiveless malignity without the malignity.

26. BAMBOO BLINDS

Once Hogen was teaching the monks before the morning meal. He pointed to the bamboo blinds. Two monks came out and rolled them up. "One wins, the other loses!" was his comment.

Comparisons are odious, but odiousness is one of the qualities—almost the chief quality—of the universe. Zen means not choosing, not praising or blaming, not liking or loathing—so they say. But real Zen means choosing, praising, blaming, liking, loathing—humorously. One wins, and rejoices, another loses and weeps. We, as Paul says, rejoice with him that rejoices, and weep with him that weeps; but don't take either too seriously.

27. MAY I ASK?

A monk said to Seppo, "The seeing into this nature of a Sravaka is like gazing at the moon at night; a bodhisattvas seeing into his nature is like the sun in the day-time. "May I ask what your seeing into your nature was like?" Seppo struck him three times with his stick. Afterwards the monk went to Ganto and asked him the same question. Ganto cuffed him three times.

To ask another person about his satori is like asking how much money he has in the bank, or whether he loves his wife. Good manners applies to all things without distinction. Indeed, Zen is good taste, or rather, good taste is Zen. Perhaps, after all, beating and slapping is the only way of improving a person's taste, religious and artistic. This is the profound meaning of existentialism. The more we suffer, intelligently, the deeper our life. Buddha said that life is suffering, and taught us how to avoid both. This was wrong. Deep suffering is deep life. Shall we then be shallow, and dry up altogether?

28. STRIKING THE POST

Hofuku, seeing a monk, struck the (round) out-side post of the temple; he then struck the head of the monk, who cried out with pain. Hofuku said, "Why doesn't the post feel pain?" The monk gave no answer.

The answer is: "The question is the same as, 'Have you stopped beating your wife?' " In other words, the answer to the question why the post doesn't feel pain, is, "It does." "Why doesn't it cry out, then?" "It does." "Why don't I hear it?" "You do, but you don't know you do." "Why don't I know?" "Because you are not enlightened." "Why am I not enlightened?" "Because you are too damn lazy!" "Why . . ."

29. WHERE ARE YOU GOING?

A monk was saying farewell to Joshu, who asked him, "Where are you going?" The monk said, "All over the place, to learn Buddhism." Joshu said, holding up his mosquito-swatter, "Do not stay where the Buddha is! Pass quickly through a place where there is no Buddha! Do not make a mistake and bring up Buddhism to anyone for three thou-sand leagues!" The monk said, "In that case I won't go!" Joshu said, "Farewell! Farewell!"

The mistake of looking for Buddhism, for Zen,

for truth, reality, God, apart from this thing at this place at this moment is so ineradicable as to make us think sometimes that perhaps after all God is up there in the sky, and reality is a big block of Something that we must nibble at, and the truth something that must be sought with shoes shod with iron. But as Stevenson said of the touchstone, "What if it was in his pocket all the time?"

30. THE DEEPEST

Dogo was asked by a monk, "What is the deepest?" Dogo came down from his seat, made obeisance in the manner of women, and said, "You have come from far, and I have no answer for you."

Dogo's action and words were deepest. To know that there is nothing to know, and to grieve that it is so difficult to communicate this "nothing to know" to others—this is the life of Zen, this is the deepest thing in the world.

31. MOSQUITO BRUSH

A monk asked Gensha, "The old masters, when they raised the gavel or lifted up the mosquito brush—did they thus bring out the essence of Zen?" "They did not," said Gensha. The monk

then asked, "What was the meaning of their ac-
tions?" Gensha raised his mosquito brush. The
monk asked, "What is the essence of Zen?" Gensha
said, "When you are enlightened you will know."

Have all men the Buddha nature? What is the
Buddha nature? The Buddha nature is to know
(potentially, subconsciously, in practice) that we
have the Buddha nature, to know too when we
ask questions, that they are foolish, and the answers to them more so. This "knowing" is not that
something is known; something is always about to
be known. We are eternally just going to have the
Buddha nature. We haven't exactly not got it, but
not exactly have it. To go back to the original
question: have all men the Buddha nature? We
may ask a second question, a question which is
more congruent with the first than most people
suspect; have all men a sense of poetry, a sense of
humor? If we answer yes, we look like fools; if no,
ill-natured. Gensha answers, "If and when." The
Christian religion says that some cannot be saved,
either by the will of God (Calvinism) or by their
own.

32. CHANGING BUDDHA

*Joshua said to his monks, "A clay Buddha won't
pass through water; an iron Buddha won't pass
through a furnace; a wooden Buddha won't pass
through a fire."*

This does not mean that the Buddha is something spiritual. It does not mean "Lay not up treasures for yourselves on earth, but lay up for yourselves treasures in heaven." It does not mean put your mind nowhere, on nothing. It means that you must be the changeless water, the furnace, the fire, through which all things must pass and change. It means that you must be clay, the iron, the wooden Buddha, and change with them.

33. A LADLEFUL

Kankei said, "When I was with Rinzai I got a ladleful, and when I was with Massan a ladleful." He added, "It is all open and unhidden in the ten directions, not a gate on the four sides, completely clear, without any attachment to anything at all, no place to take hold of it."

This is one of the best definitions of Zen. We get a ladleful of it here and there according to our (accidental) innate abilities, and our (accidental) opportunities. But what the ladle is full of we cannot put into *other* words. It is just a ladleful of Zen.

34. WEARING CLOTHES, EATING FOOD

A monk said to Bokushu, "We are always putting on and taking off our clothes, and eating our food—is there any way of avoiding this?" Bokushu said, "By putting on and taking off our clothes, and eating our food." The monk said, "I don't understand." Bokushu said, "Not understanding is wearing clothes, eating food."

Rightly enough, we get tired of doing things mechanically—when we think of it. Breathing and the beating of the heart we are tired of when we are dead. We must enjoy all we do, consciously or unconsciously. Thus, not to understand is the (happy) wearing of clothes, the (happy) eating of food. And if we have the (Zen) understanding of the matter, the wearing and the eating are a non-wearing and a non-eating, or, as Bokushu says at the beginning, the (Zen) avoiding of wearing and eating—that is, wearing and eating.

35. VULGAR CREATURE

One day Rinzai was out and begging and came to the house of a well-off man. He said, "Another bowl more than usual, please!" An old woman came to the door and said, "What a vulgar, greedy creature!" Rinzai said, "I don't see the slightest sign of food—where is the vulgarity and greediness?" The old woman shut the door in his face.

Rinzai asked for more food to test the person of the house. The old woman, knowing something of Zen, returned the attack. Rinzai then spiritualizes the matter, like Christ with the woman at the well, but the old woman sees Rinzai is too strong for her, and finds discretion is the better part of valor. The Jewish woman at the well is a Buddhist. The old Chinese woman is not.

36. WOODEN BALL

One day Seppo sat down on his seat, and all the monks assembled, and Seppo rolled along a wooden ball. Gensha went after it, and put it back in its original place.

To roll a ball is to see the ballness of the ball, its woodenness; and the woodenness, the levelness of the floor; the roundness of the earth, its pull-fulness; the desire of the ball to roll, its desire to stop rolling. But besides this spontaneous willfulness of nature there is the thoughtful control, the orderliness, the infinite finality of man. In these two, which work together undivided, yet always separately, as in Seppo and Gensha, is seen Universal Activity, the Buddha nature, Godhead.

37. TRUE EYE

A monk asked, "What is the True Eye of the Law?" Chokei said, "I have a favor to ask of you: don't throw sand around!"

People ask why and how as an excuse for not doing what they know they should do. In some ways illusion, as Nietzsche said, is life-giving, and we may tell a lie until it becomes the truth, but such truths are not fundamental. We have to learn to look with the eye, and the only way is to keep on looking, looking at a snake until it ceases to be repulsive, looking at a naked woman until she ceases to be attractive, and until snakes and women become supremely interesting.

38. EGGPLANT ROOTS

A monk said to Basho, "How about before the ancient Buddhas appeared on earth?" Basho said, "A thousand years of eggplant roots." The monk asked, "How about after they appeared?" Basho said, "The Deva Kings roll their eyes violently."

Before Buddhism, we are animals, one almost might say vegetables, with no value or use. After Buddhism we are afraid to sin, afraid of not being enlightened.

39. NO QUESTIONS!

One day while Gensha was thinking, he heard the voice of a swallow, and said, "How well it has explained the Buddhist Truth, speaking profoundly of the Real Nature of Things!" and came down from his seat. Afterwards a monk, wishing to get some profit from his words, said to Gensha, "I didn't understand what you meant." Gensha retorted, "Be off with you! How can anyone trust you!"

I have been asked many questions in my life about poetry, religion, life, and I have given precisely the same number of answers, but I have never, I repeat, *never*, satisfied a single interlocutor. Why was this? Because all questioning is a way of avoiding the real answer, which, as Zen tells us, is really known already. Every man is enlightened, but wishes he wasn't. Every man knows he must love his enemies, and sell all he has and give to the poor, but he doesn't wish to know it—so he asks questions. Gensha's reply to the questioner is too kind; he should just say, "Liar!"

40. HOW'S THE GRUEL?

Sozan asked a monk where he had come from. He replied, "From Seppo." Sozan said, "When you were here before, you were not satisfied; how about now?" "Now I am satisfied," said the monk. Sozan asked, "Satisfied with the gruel, satisfied with the rice?" The monk made no reply.

Sozan's last question is not merely sarcastic. The question is not whether we are spiritually satisfied or not but materially. If we are satisfied materially we are really satisfied. If we like the gruel, and don't mind if it is a bit burnt, or has too much salt in it—this is Paradise, this is Nirvana, this is Zen. If, however, we are satisfied about our hopes of heaven, but grumble about the food, this is Hell, this is illusion, this un-Zen. When the monk was asked the question about the gruel and the rice, he should have answered, "I am satisfied with it, and with no gruel, and to be drowned in gruel!"

41. THE SUPREME DOCTRINE

A monk asked Gensha, "The Supreme Doctrine— is there any explanation of it recently?" Gensha said, "We don't hear such a thing often."

This grim understatement nullifies all the books on Zen that ever were or will be written. Zen is how things are said, or heard, but also how they are not said, and "those unheard are sweeter." To talk with Zen is not uncommon, and talking abut Zen is more common than it should be, but to talk with Zen about Zen—it is the rarest thing in the world.

42. MAD ABOUT RABBITS!

Joshu and an attendant were walking about the garden when a rabbit ran past them. The attendant said to him, "You are a great and good man;

*what do you see when a rabbit runs by?" Joshu
said, "I'm mad about rabbits!"*

This is not quite the same as the White Rabbit
that ran past Alice, but it is equally and intensely
interesting. This is the (Shakespearean) answer
that we should give to a question about everything: "I'm mad about it!" This is the life of Zen.

43. ABSENCE OF GOODNESS

*A monk said to Seppo, "I have shaved my head,
put on black clothes, received the vows—why am I
not to be considered a Buddha?" Seppo said,
"There is nothing better than an absence of goodness."*

The difference between religion and morality,
between poetry and emotion, between music and
sentimentality, lives here. "Judge not" is usually
taken to mean, "Do not condemn others," because
you will be yourself condemned. "Judge not"
means, "Do not judge your own actions or those
of others good or bad, approve or disapprove of
them." We must have no principles, no standards,
no values. It is true that everything thus becomes
wildly subjective, but it can't be helped. You must
believe that your real nature is no different from
the nature of things, and must somehow try to get
at it. This is how, Seppo says, you may become a
Buddha.

44. ONE IN THE HALL

A monk asked Joshu, "What is the Buddha?"
"The one in the Hall." The monk said, "The one
in the Hall is a statue, a lump of mud!" Joshu
said, "That is so." "What is the Buddha?" asked
the monk. "The one in the Hall."

This becomes easier, perhaps, if expressed a
little more paradoxically. Even the clay statue of a
man who lived a thousand years ago (from that
time) is the Buddha. What indeed is not the Buddha? Even the Buddha was a Buddha.

45. WATER-FIRE

A monk asked Hofuku, "How can we enter the
fire and not be burned, enter the water and not be
drowned?" Hofuku said, "If it were water-fire,
would you be burned-drowned?"

This ingenious answer means that we are
scorched to death, or drowned to death, because
we distinguish fire and water. We die because we
distinguish life and death.

46. HAIR'S BREADTH DIFFERENCE

A monk asked Joshu, "A hair's breadth of differ-
ence—and what happens?" Joshu answered,

"Heaven and earth are far away." The monk said,
"And when there is not a hair's breadth of differ-
ence?" Joshu said, "Heaven and earth are far
away."

The monk and Joshu are quoting from the
Hsinhsinming. But Joshu goes beyond it, in assert-
ing that with satori or without it, the world is unchanged. This is not mere contradictoriness, but
the transcendence of all assertions. The assertion is
all right, *if it is, at the same moment, transcended
as well.* An assertion is nothing; transcending it is
nothing; the two together is Something.

47. I LIT THE FIRE

*Kassan had a monk who went round all the Zen
temples but found nothing to suit him anywhere.
The name of Kassan, however, was often men-
tioned to him from far and near as a great master,
so he came back and interviewed Kassan, and said,
"You have an especial understanding of Zen. How
is it you didn't reveal this to me?" Kassan said,
"When you boiled rice, didn't I light the fire?
When you passed round the food, didn't I offer
my bowl to you? When did I betray your expecta-
tions?" The monk was enlightened.*

We teach Zen, if we teach it at all, by the way
we write, the way we light the fire, or hold out
the bowl to be filled with rice. It is also true, how-

ever, that there may be some intellectual obstacle which prevents the (physical) eye or ear or nose from perceiving truth directly. In such a case, the meaning, the intellectual meaning of the words, may cause satori, in the sense of removing that intellectual obstacle. In the present case, the monk, who is called "a small master," realized intellectually that he had made a mistake in doing the round of the Zen masters expecting to get something from them, or from Kassan himself.

48. DEEP MOUNTAINS

One day Gensha said, "In the deep mountains and inaccessible peaks where for a thousand years, for ten thousand years no man has ever trod, can we find Buddhism there or not? If you say yes, what kind of Buddhism is it? And if you say no, then Buddhism is not universal."

This is indeed a dilemma, perhaps *the* dilemma. No, is the common-sense answer. Yes, is the pantheistic, and the (false) Zen answer. The only reply we can give is the opposite to that expected, and the opposite to the one we gave the day before. But to say, like Buddha, that such questions are not conducive to the good life and should not be asked—this is untrue. They must be asked, vehemently, and answered, vehemently. That is why Gensha asked his question.

49. THE HALL'S FALLING DOWN!

Yakusan's manner of death was of a piece with his life. When he was about to die, he yelled out, "The Hall's falling down! The Hall's falling down!" The monks brought various things and began to prop it up. Yakusan threw up his hands and said, "None of you understood what I meant!" and died.

What did Yakusan mean? Everything is falling down; everything is rising up. To prop what must fall is foolish; rather, give it a push. When some famous work of art or monument of culture is destroyed, when a moth is burnt in a flame, when five million Jews are slaughtered, let us do what Yakusan did—yell, and die.

50. THE ZEN SWORD

A monk asked Chokoman, "What is this sword that will cut a hair that is blown onto it?" Chokoman said, "You can't touch it." The monk asked, "How about one who uses it?" "His bones and body are smashed to smithereens," said Chokoman. "Then," said the monk, "it's a jolly good thing not to be able to touch it!" Chokoman struck him.

The sword is Zen, which no one can hold, and if he does, he loses his life; he is crucified on the cross of this world. So the monk says, "Let us eat, drink, and be merry, for tomorrow we die," and Chokoman hits him, because he wants him to die now—now or never!

3. ANALYSIS

**Cases from the *Mumonkan*
with modern interpretations**

WHY NO BEARD?

THE CASE

Wakuan said, "Why has the Western Barbarian (Bodhidharma) no beard?"

Some commentators take this to mean, "Why has the beardless foreigner no beard?" This is certainly a difficult question to answer unscientifically, and worthy of a Zen master, but a more natural interpretation is, "Why has the bearded foreigner no beard?" Indians and Persians were usually hairy people compared to the (Southern) Chinese, whose beard often consisted of a few long black hairs.

The problem Wakuan sets us is not a philosophical or in the ordinary sense a religious one. Christ was a man; he was also God. Mary was a virgin, and a mother at the same time. God created the world out of nothing. God is the author of evil, but not responsible for it. He creates imperfection, but is himself perfect. Christ died for mankind, but is far from really dead. All this is no different from a beardless bearded barbarian. The great difference between Zen and Christianity, however, is this—that Zen does not ask us somehow or other to believe in the contradiction. It requires us to become the omnipotent weak Nazarene. We have ourselves to create the universe out of nothing, to have a virgin birth, to be perfectly imperfect, to have a beard and not to have it, all at the same time.

THE COMMENTARY

If you study Zen, you must really study it. If you become enlightened it must be the real enlightenment. If you once see the barbarian's real face intimately, then you have at last got "it." But when you explain what you saw, you have already fallen into relativity.

Once I stayed for some time at a small Zen temple. I got up at the proper time, 4:30 A.M. and cleaned the temple every day, but the monks were all in bed until seven or eight o'clock. I cursed them as I swept, and despised them as I washed the floor. I hoped the roshi would get up and catch them slacking and find me heroically working in the darkness, but he never did. He was in bed himself. I judged the monks indifferent to their duty and to the welfare and prosperity of Zen. I thought of nothing else but them and their idleness, and begrudged both my own labor and their slumbers. Some time after, hearing of this from me, the roshi asked, "For whose sake do you clean the temple?" This question was a puzzler. He himself answered, "For your own sake. When you work, work for yourself, not for other people." When you work, just work, don't worry about whether others are working, or whether the temple will be burned down next week or not. When you sleep, just sleep, don't worry about whether your beard is in the bed or outside. When you write a book, don't worry about whether it will ever be published or whether anyone will ever read it. All that is God's worry. Let him worry about it. This is the meaning of "casting all your care upon him." Why did Daruma have a beard? Why did he have no beard? Why did he have five and a half beards? Here is the first step toward the answer.

THE VERSE

> Before a fool,
> Do not expound your dream.
> The beardless barbarian—
> It is adding obscurity to clarity!

The first two lines seem to have something of the meaning of "Cast not your pearls before swine," one of the least agreeable sayings attributed to Christ. It is certainly a waste of time to express our experiences of truth to others, unless, like Shakespeare or Homer, we have the power to universalize them, that is, somehow show others that they have actually had the same experiences. What we can do, then, is always take the opportunity of drawing other people's attention to their own possession of pearls, that is, their experiences of reality. We ourselves often do, as Emerson says, neglect our own intuitions and have to "receive them with shame from another." In any case, "Quench not the spirit!" is the motto, as Kierkegaard says.

The second two lines of the verse are a sort of short history of the world, or at least of religion. Our ordinary life is a kind of, not mixture, but alloy of absolute and relative. When we begin to distinguish the two, we become exceedingly confused. Which are we to believe, "Death before dishonor," or "Safety first"? Ultimately we come to see that these two, this so-called alloy, was not composed of two things at all, that they were all the time identical, that the "real" table and the table we eat our dinner on is the same table. The table is square; at the same time it is round. Daruma has a beard; at the same time he has no beard. Every thing is relative; at the same time it is absolute. "God is not a God of the dead, but of the living, for unto Him all live." This is true, but not the whole truth, because unto God the dead are also dead, and the living living. There is not a relative truth, *and* an absolute truth. The relative is the absolute, the absolute is the relative, and yet we must go on and assert that the relative is not only the absolute but the relative; the absolute is not only the relative but the absolute. However we synthesize, and say "Difference is sameness, and sameness is difference," we must continue to analyze, and say that difference is not sameness, and sameness is not difference. And is not all this "adding the obscurity of thought to the clarity and simplicity of daily life?" It is; but thus, and by no other means, we become human.

KYOGEN'S MAN-UP-A-TREE

THE CASE

Kyogen said, "It's like a man (a monk) up a tree, hanging from a branch with his mouth; his hands can't grasp a bough, his feet won't reach one. Under the tree there is another man, who asks him the meaning of Daruma's coming from the West. If he doesn't answer, he evades his duty. If he answers, he will lose his life. What should he do?"

This problem is a central one in human life, particularly between teacher and pupil, husband and wife, and so on. If we teach, they don't understand. If we don't teach, they are dissatisfied. Love is mutual obedience. Also it means teaching the other to love more. If I am always obedient, the other becomes impudent or at least makes no progress. If I demand obedience, love being mutual, the other's love simply decreases. Kierkegaard says that we must believe in the love in the other's heart and thus arouse it. Perhaps this is the answer to Kyogen's problem, but we must not expect any results. Simply believe, believe that if we open our mouths we won't fall, believe that if we don't open our mouths the other will somehow understand by that the meaning of the coming of Daruma from the West.

THE COMMENTARY

Though your eloquence flows like a river, it is all of no avail. Even if you can explain the whole body of the Buddhist sutras, that also is useless. If you can answer the problem properly, you can kill the living, bring the dead to life. But if you can't answer, you must ask Maitreya when he comes.

"Though I should speak with the tongues of men and angels, and have not charity ..." What is charity? Is it perhaps the answer to Kyogen's question? If we really love somebody or some animal or plant, that is enough. Lovingly shutting the mouth or lovingly opening it, lovingly living, lovingly dying—that is Zen.

The whole corpus of the Buddhist scripture was first made in China in A.D. 581. Buddha would have read his sutras with surprise, and perhaps not have understood many of them, especially perhaps the *Platform Sutra*, written by a Chinese. In any case, it is important not to despise words. Actions, it is said, speak louder, but not less truly, not more untruly.

In the last sentence of the Commentary, Mumon is threatening the reader with the results of a lack of seriousness in grasping the meaning of the problem. Maitreya is the next Buddha, now in

the Tusita Heaven. He is to come 5,000 years
(others say 5,670,000,000 years) after the Nirvana
of Sakyamuni.

THE VERSE

Kyogen really has bad taste,
And spreads poison limitlessly.
He stops up the monks' mouths,
And frantically they squeeze tears out from
*   their dead eyes.*

Mumon is praising Kyogen in reverse, or rather
he is showing us that as far as profit and loss are
concerned, there is never one without the other.
This is Emerson's compensation. And indeed he
may pose another problem. Suppose a man practices asceticism for ten years, and the day before
he is going to be enlightened, he dies! Was it
worth it all? Would it not have been better to
read poetry, listen to Bach, enjoy the four seasons,
"Flowers in the summer, fires in the fall." The orthodox will say that he will get enlightenment
very soon and easily in the next life, but there's no
end to nonsense. Anyway Mumon is talking like
the schoolboy who regrets that such people as Eu-
clid and Shakespeare were ever born. Another
way of thinking of Mumon's aspersions on Kyogen
is, "Damn braces, bless relaxes." When words are
the flower of action, continuous with it, all is well,
but afterwards, when we repeat them, they hide

more truth than they reveal, and to meaningfulize them we are forced to say the opposite of what was said before, to curse where we blessed, to make alive what we destroyed.

THE BUDDHA'S FLOWER

THE CASE

Once when the World-Honored One, in ancient times, was upon Mount Grdhrakuta, he held up a flower before the congregation of monks. At this time all were silent, but the Venerable Kasyapa only smiled. The World-Honored One said, "I have the Eye of the True Law, the Secret Essence of Nirvana, the Formless Form, the Mysterious Law-Gate. Without relying upon words and letters, beyond all teaching as a special transmission, I pass this all on to Mahakasyapa."

"The wonderful gate of the law" means the mysterious but everyday power by which with words or with no words we arouse the deepest spiritual-material truths in our common minds, as Buddha did between himself and Kasyapa. This has more or less the same meaning as, "A special transmission outside the scriptures." As for "No dependence upon words and letters," the existence of the *Mumonkan* itself shows that this statement really means that all words are misleading except Zen words; but so are all actions. Buddha's holding up the flower—has this the meaning of Christ's "Consider the lilies of the field"? We are told to

119

consider how they grow, without intellectuality, without emotion, without hope or satiety. The result is a beauty, a significance greater than the most successful human life. Was Buddha's flower Tennyson's "in the crannied wall" that revealed to Mahakasyapa "what God and man is"? Eckhart says:

> The meanest thing that one knows in God—for instance, if one could understand a flower as it has its being in God; this would be a higher thing than the whole world!

Then there is the *Immortality Ode*:

> To me the meanest flower that blows
> Can give thoughts that lie too deep for tears.

The trouble, and what Zen wishes us to avoid, is the dividing of the flower and its meaning, the flower and "the thoughts that wander through eternity." When "the bright consummate flower" is really seen, the flower sees itself. The self flowers.

THE COMMENTARY

Golden-faced Kudon impudently forced the good people into depravity. Advertising sheep's heads, he sells dog-flesh—but with some genius. However, supposing that at that time all the monks had laughed, how would the "all-including

eye of the absolute truth" have been handed on?
Or if Kasyapa had not smiled, how would it have
been handed on? If you say, it can (anyway) be
handed on, that's the Golden-faced Old Huckster
with his loud-voiced swindling at the town gate.
If you say it can't, why did Buddha say he had
handed it on to Kasyapa?

"Golden-faced" has many explanations. Sakyamuni was born in Kapilavastu; *kapila* means
brown. The people of his tribe were called "yel-
low-faced" because of the color of their skins. The
statues of Buddha were of gold, or covered with
gold-foil. Kudon is a transliteration of Gautama,
one of Buddha's names before his enlightenment.

"Advertising sheep's heads," and so on, may be
taken as praising of Buddha with faint damns, but
Mumon's constant object is to prevent us from
forming any dogmatic principle, from coming to
any conclusion, from being able to say "I understand!" Again, in the last part, he uses logic to put
us in a quandary as to whether and when and how
the "truth" is transmitted from one person to
another. Even Mumon himself does not ask or
answer the question, "What if the line of transmission had been broken?" But we must answer
it, and not fall into either nihilism or superstition.

THE VERSE

> *Holding up a flower,*
> *The snake shows his tail.*
> *Kasyapa smiles,*
> *The monks don't know what to do.*

The snake shows his tail only; the Buddha holds up only a single flower, but the Ophidia and Flora are grasped. The part is greater than the whole. When Buddha holds up a flower some monks should dance round it, some make a sketch of it, some grind it underfoot, some spit on it—all according to their free-moving life. It would be a great mistake to think that Kasyapa smiled as a sign that he understood something or other. His "breaking his face" was the opening of the flower. We must weep with those that weep, and rejoice with those that rejoice.

JOSHU'S BOWL WASHING

THE CASE

A monk said to Joshu, "I have just entered this monastery. I beg you to teach me." Joshu asked, "Have you eaten your rice-gruel?" "I have," replied the monk. "Then," said Joshu, "go and wash your bowl(s)." The monk was enlightened.

This Case looks easy, but cannot be (intellectually) solved. Zen means doing ordinary things willingly and cheerfully. Zen is common life and uncommon life, sense and transcendence, both as one, yet two. When the monk heard what Joshu said, he saw his rice bowl as "that upturned bowl we call the sky." But we need to insert some humor in it, and when Joshu said, "Wash your bowl, that's all!" he meant, "Wash your bowl, that's All." Or he meant,

> Washing is truth, truth washing; that is all
> Ye know on earth, and all ye need to know.

The great danger is to divide the washing and the truth.

> Sweeping a room as for thy laws
> Makes that and the action fine.

This is true. The room is well swept; the sweeping is well done, but the "as" is too separative to allow us to call these lines of Herbert an expression of Zen. Wash away your dirty enlightenment; sweep away the divinity, and even the fineness.

THE COMMENTARY

Joshu opened his mouth and showed his gallbladder, his heart, and his liver. If the monk didn't really grasp the truth, he mistook the bell for a pot.

There are actually three mistakes we can make. We can look at things in the common-sense way, or the transcendental, or the symbolical. With the present anecdote, the danger is in the first and the third. Zen is not simply doing everything with all one's heart and soul. "Your ordinary mind—that is the Way." This is true, but not when understood in a pedestrian manner. A bowl must be washed religiously, but with no feeling of the holiness of the action. The washing of the bowl does not "mean" the washing away of the idea of enlightenment. If Joshu had asked the monk if he had washed his bowl, and said, "Then put some rice in it!" there is no difference. The Sixth Patriarch Eno was especially insistent on this, in reference to Jinshu's saying that we must keep the mirror of our hearts bright and clean, and allow no dust to fall on it. It is true, in a way, that we must not desire anything, especially desire enlightenment, but Eno says that the "must not" is wrong. You must not say "must not." Joshu is pointing to this contradictory realm in which there is no common sense, no transcendence, no symbolism. *Pilgrim's Progress* tells us of the man with a muck-rake, a golden crown hanging unseen over his head. This is the human situation, but at the same time we have a golden-crown-rake, with muck hanging unseen over our heads.

THE VERSE

> *He has made it all so clear,*
> *It takes a long time to catch the point.*
> *If you realize that it's foolish to look for*
> *   fire with a fire,*
> *The meal won't take so long to cook.*

To say, "Then wash your bowl!" is indeed too simple, yet the more we explain, the worse it gets. The short-cut, or the long way round—both have their disadvantages. We are always complicated about simple things, like Hamlet, or simple about complicated things, like Othello.

The second two lines have the same meaning as the drowning man begging for water, and the rich man's son dying of poverty in *Hakuin Zenji's Wasan*. If the bird began to look for the air, or the fish for the water—but are these similes any use? What is difficult to grasp is that the bird is the air, and the fish is the water, and at the same time they are utterly different from each other. The whole problem lies in "at the same time."

TOZAN'S STRIPES

THE CASE

Tozan came to learn from Ummon, and was asked by him, "Where have you come from?" "From Sato," he replied. "Where were you during the summer?" "I was at Hoji Temple in Konan Province." "When did you leave there?" "On the twenty-fifth of August." Ummon burst out, "A beating is what you want!" The next day Tozan came and knelt before Ummon, and said, "Yesterday I was (to be) beaten by you. I did and said nothing I shouldn't. What did I do wrong?" Ummon said, "You dirty big belly bag! What did you come from Kozei and Konan for?" Suddenly Tozan came to a realization.

No doubt Tozan thought he had done something good and meritorious in traveling all those hundreds of miles to receive the mysterious Truth from a real teacher, but it was just this very point, the very thing for which he might have received a medal, that Ummon picked on to curse him for. It is not so much our sins, which are obvious weakness and vulgarity, as our virtures that we need to be delivered from. Even if the Rich Young Man had given up all his wealth to feed the poor he would still be farther from Heaven than Judas or Ananias. "Forgive us our good deeds, as we forgive those who do good deeds to us."

Tozan, confronted by a Man, Ummon, behaved like the swine before pearls. He spoke of Ummon as though he were an ordinary man, hardened in superficialities, in news, in gossip, in trivial things like the annihilation of mankind, or how to get rich quick. The most dangerous thing in the world is to think you understand something. Running all over China, or all through the Bible is no help.

The beating that Tozan received was different from ordinary beatings; he did not feel Ummon was doing it to teach him something, or for his good. It was just Nature beating him. "The Lord hath given pain; the Lord hath taken away pain; blessed be the name of the Lord!"

THE COMMENTARY

If Ummon at that time, by giving him the fodder of the sect, had shown him that One Way of Living Activity, it would not have become extinct.

All night Tozan wallowed in the waves of the sea of Yes and No until he could get nowhere, and, when long-awaited dawn broke, again went to Ummon, and had his eyes opened by him, and was suddenly enlightened, but he was not a seasoned man yet.

Now I ask all of you: Was Tozan's being beaten

right or wrong? If it was right, then everything in the universe should be beaten; if it was wrong, then Ummon was a swindler. If you understand this clearly, then you and Tozan breathe the same air.

The "fodder" is the blows and shattering cries (almost war whoops) of the Sect.

Mumon makes a serious charge here that Ummon, by his weakness, in not shouting and beating more, not only did not give Tozan the opportunity for a deeper enlightenment, but in the end brought about the extinction of his own Branch of Zen. This latter was due partly to Ummon's willfulness and eccentricity, in other words his genius, and this is not entirely unconnected with beating people and shouting at them less than more mediocre Zen masters.

Mumon's question about Ummon being right or wrong in beating Tozan reminds us of Hamlet's "Use every man after his desert, and who should 'scape whipping?" No man has the right or duty to strike any other person, or even a fly. On the other hand, every thing in the world must be beaten, and is in fact always being beaten. This is the meaning of what Pater says in *Marius the Epicurean*, the double feeling we have which is deeper than the Zen resolving of it:

> He could not kill the snakes, for they already suffered, in being what they were.

THE VERSE

The lion has a roundabout way of teach-
ing her cubs.
Intending to urge them on, she kicks
them away,
And they soon redress themselves and
charge back.
Heedlessly he came back to Ummon but
was checkmated;
The first arrow was only a scratch, but
the second one went deep.

This is rather feeble, and Mumon seems to be praising Ummon here. "Checkmated" means by calling Tozan a "full-belly." "The first arrow" was beating him, the second arrow was showing Tozan that there is Someone who does not go from place to place, who is without shadow of turning, and this is Tozan himself.

ECHU'S THREE CALLS

THE CASE

The National Teacher called the attendant three times, and three times he answered. The National Teacher said, "I thought I had transgressed against you, but it seems that you transgressed against me."

When one person calls to another, he calls as one man to another man; or as one Buddha to another Buddha. Something in his manner or tone of voice shows clearly which it is. If I have been listening to Bach (when it is played properly) and I say to someone, "How was it?" I speak as a Buddha, to a Buddha, of a Buddha. When I receive my salary, the reverse is the case, though this of course is not proper, since money is necessary not only for life but for the music of Bach itself.

The words of Echu may be taken in this way. "I thought your lack of enlightenment was due to the poorness of my teaching (calling), but I see that you are lacking in earnestness and zeal by the ordinariness of your responses." To put the same thing in a different way, "All the sin and confusion of the world is due to my own sin and confusion, for I and others are one thing. But in the same way you are responsible for it all, for you and others are one thing." There is a democracy of responsibility, an equality of transgression, a fraternity of impotence which is also a precarious, a human thing.

Another way of looking at the matter is this. Echu calls Oshin. "Somewhere a voice is calling." Someone calls, we think, someone is called. But as Lao-tse says, the real person is nameless, egoless, soul-less, person-less, somebody-less. Echu is "realizing" this as he calls Oshin. Oshin is wrong to answer, but Echu was wrong to call. God should not have created the world in the first place. That was the Big Mistake which mankind is even now trying to rectify with a big bomb. Thus the Case is a joke, but it needs a very strong and delicate sense of humor to perceive this kind of cosmic joke.

THE COMMENTARY

The National Teacher called three times. His tongue fell to the ground (from talking too much). The attendant answered three times, sending out a corresponding glory. The National Teacher, getting old and lonely, pushed the cow's head down to the grass. The attendant would have none of it; delicious food is not suitable for a man who is satiated. Just say, in what did the transgressing consist? When the country is prosperous, rich children are too proud (to eat plain food).

In this period, the eighth century, Buddhism and Zen were popular, and masters and disciples became indolent like Echu and Oshin, just calling to each other and answering.

What was the transgression? Commentators do not attempt to explain, fearing, no doubt, that the mocking ghost of Mumon will haunt them for the temerarious wallowing in relativity. The answer is, the fall of things into consciousness, and again into self-consciousness. To live is to transgress. To err is (to be a) human (being). This is part of what Buddha realized under the Bodhi tree. "The wages of sin, that is, of life, is death." Death without life is impossible. Nirvana is release from life, from life and death, calling and answering. This was the Indian, the Buddhist idea.

The Zen, the Chinese experience was that this was only half Nirvana. The other half was not to be released from life and death, from calling and answering. So we must call as not calling, not call as calling, answer as not answering, not answer as answering—a tall order, indeed, and how many, many years it must take even to approach this condition.

THE VERSE

He must carry the hole-less iron cangue,
And his decendants too can have no peace or
rest.
If you wish to support your religion and cause
it to flourish

You must climb a mountain of swords with bare feet.

A wooden cangue, with a hole in it for the head, can be borne, but a heavy iron one, with no hole in it at all, is something we see in dreams only. An iron flute with no holes in it is another Zen metaphor of something the intellect cannot deal with.

What Mumon says here is not very different from Kierkegaard's emendation of Christ's words into, "Narrowness is the Way." However, Mumon, though often sadistic, seems to have very little masochism, and is saying that the painfulness of the experience is necessary for the deepening of life. What does this mean for our actual life? Are we to sin that grace may abound? Are we to seek occasions for grief over and above those which heredity and chance bring us? Not directly, of course, but by making ourselves, or allowing ourselves to become more and more sensitive to more and more things. Here is a man, a cockroach, a matchstick, a distant lamp; Christ died in blood for these; Buddha sweated under a tree for them; Echu called to them; Oshin answered them.

The illustration of the cangue is a happy one. It is a large square slab of wood made in two parts locked together round the criminal's neck. We all wear the cangue of relativity, and the punishment is made to fit the crime. When we study Zen, however, we find ourselves with the same old cangue, but there is a difference. It has no hole in it (the calling and the answering have nothing between them). It doesn't fit us. It is heavier than before;

we are more uncomfortable than ordinary people, who are pretty used to theirs, who are usually proud of it, and often decorate it with medals and badges.

TOZAN'S FLAX

THE CASE

A monk asked Tozan, "What is the Buddha?"
He replied, "Three pounds of flax."

What the Buddha is, is the most difficult question man can ask. What is God? What is Truth? What is Life? What is the Universe? These, all these together make up the monk's question. Tozan's answer comes then as a kind of anticlimax, too absurd to be serious, and if it does not make you laugh when you hear it, you are in a bad way indeed, for as Blake said, "No man can see truth without believing it," and who can see truth without joy and laughter?

We should note the lack of vagueness in the answer. It is not any amount of flax, but three pounds, no more, no less; not three pounds of anything, but three pounds of flax. The questioning monk knew, or thought he knew, that everything in the world was the Buddha. Like the Rich Young Ruler, only one thing was lacking—this three pounds of flax. But it is not that this three pounds of flax also is the Buddha. It is the Dharmakaya and the Sambhogakaya and Nirmanakaya with nothing omitted.

Some people say that Tozan was himself weighing the flax or was watching or overheard someone else doing it. Or perhaps it just came into his mind fortuitously, something out of his childhood. It makes no difference. The Buddha is not Tozan or the monk. He is not three pounds of flax. He is "three pounds of flax." Expressed scientifically, the Buddha is "   ," sometimes.

THE COMMENTARY

Old Tozan's Zen is rather like a clam; when it just opens the two halves of the shell, you can see the liver and the intestines. But though this may be so, just say, where can we see Tozan?

After all, the real secrets are what everybody knows. As Confucius said, "To know that you know, and to know that you don't know—that is the real wisdom." The wages of sin is death, but nobody knows it. All flesh is grass, but nobody knows it. God is love, but nobody knows it. Bach is the only musician ever born, but nobody knows it. "A little flower is the labor of ages," but nobody knows it. The Buddha is three pounds of flax, but nobody knows it.

Mumon asks, "Where can we see [the real] Tozan?" This is a new question. What is the difference between the Buddha, alias three pounds of flax, and Tozan? If it is the real Tozan and the Buddha, the answer is, none. So the question resolves itself into, what is the difference between

Tozan and the real Tozan? We see now that Tozan's answer to the monk was wrong, or rather, in-
complete. He should have said, "Three pounds of
flax," *and*, "Any number except three, and not
pounds (ounces or tons will do) and under no circumstances flax!" That is what the Buddha really
is, and it is what Tozan is.

THE VERSE

"Three pounds of flax"—artlessly, spontaneously
  it comes out.
The words and the meaning are intimate, invisibly
  so.
He who explains this and that, yes and no, the
  relative,
Is himself [only] a relative man.

The second line shows how important words
are, how impossible it is to divide, as Keats said,
Truth and Beauty. But the "only" inserted in the
last line reminds us not to despise relativity. Without time there is no timeless. Without the three
pounds of flax there is no Buddha.

The relative speaks of the relative. The divine
speaks of the divine. Tozan spoke of the absolute,
using the words of the relative. Most people use
the words of the absolute, that is, God, immortality, eternity, infinity, but their voice is the voice of
the relative. Everything depends upon the voice,
the intonation, the inverted commas.

UMMON'S SHIT-STICK

THE CASE

A monk asked Ummon, "What is the Buddha?"
"It is a shit-wiping stick," replied Ummon.

This is my favorite Case, as Ummon is my favorite master. We have three "persons" here, Ummon, the shit-stick, and the Buddha, and difficult indeed it is to distinguish between them. Ummon was born in 966; the shit-stick with humanity; and the Buddha with the universe.

Instead of toilet paper the Chinese of this time used a piece of stick to wipe themselves after excretion. This one is a used, useless, thrown-away, dried one. This shit-stick must have been employed as a term of abuse by the common people, and no doubt such expressions could be found in other languages. Rinzai uses it of a monk who is unable to express himself. But to use it to define the Infinite, to limit the Illimitable, to equate the most worthy of things with the least, to make vessels of honor and vessels of dishonor indistinguishable, and yet not fall into indifferentism, and cynicism, to be willing to die for the lowest form of toilet paper—this is indeed *debellare superbos, parcere victis,* in a sense that should have shocked

Virgil also. To debunk the highbrow and elevate the lowbrow and bring everything into an odious middle-brow state is indeed far from Ummon's intention, but it is not altogether unconnected with it. Ummon is not teaching pantheism, nor is he even showing that all things in the world have an equal because infinite value, though to grasp this is to be more than halfway to Zen. Ummon wants us to see that this shit-stick is the whole universe, is God, is the Godhead, is Buddha. Thus it is all a question of emphasis; not, "This shit-stick is the BUDDHA!" but "THIS SHIT-STICK is the Buddha." The physical is more urgent, more lively, more explosive than the equally necessary spiritual.

THE COMMENTARY

We must say that Ummon can't appreciate plain food. He's so busy he can't even scribble properly. He is disposed to support the sect with a shit-stick. Look at the outcome!

The first two sentences mean that Ummon is careless about what he is saying because of a poverty of thought and an excessive number of disciples. The second two mean that Buddhism can be supported with money or poverty, with romanticism or bare truth, with a golden scepter or a shit-stick. Its rise or fall depends on which we choose. Build a great temple,

140

> With storied windows richly dight
> Casting a dim religious light,

form a World Buddhist Federation, have ceremonies and incense and robes and sepulchral voices and much-advertised zazen meetings—and Zen will continue—or not! Speak ill of Zen, never attend sesshin, look askance at temples, despise the masters—and Zen will . . .

THE VERSE

> *Sudden flashes of lightning!*
> *Sparks from iron striking flint!*
> *A blink of the mind's eye,*
> *And the legs are already walking in different directions.*

Ummon's shit-stick is compared to a flash of lightning and sparks in its spontaneity, thoughtlessness, wordlessness, unemotionality, lack of beauty, formlessness. In this the laconic shit-stick and the flash and the spark are like the Godhead. If the eye just for a moment becomes emotional or intellectual and feels the shit-stick repulsive, or thinks it to be unworthy of serious attention, the Buddha is lost.

BASO'S VERY MIND

THE CASE

Daibai asked Baso, "What is the Buddha?" Baso answered, "The mind is the Buddha."

When we ask, "What, who, which, where, how, when, why is the Buddha?" the form of the question already forbids the right answer. The Hsinhsinming says, "As soon as you have 'this or that,' the Mind is lost." However, it is not lost because the Buddha is everything, not merely this or that. The Hsinhsinming also says, "Do not keep to the One." Our minds, which pride themselves above all things on distinguishing good and evil, God and Devil, truth and error, by this very distinction commit a greater error than the whole-hearted embracing of the error:

If a fool would persist in his folly he would become wise.

But this is not the folly of distinguishing but the folly of not distinguishing. The word "mind" does not mean the Buddha mind, for this would make Baso's answer tautology: "The mind (or Buddha) is Buddha." Clearly "mind" means Hitler's mind, or a kangaroo's mind, or the mind of a dewdrop trembling from the eaves with "a mind to fall." It does not mean that my mind is part of the World-Soul, but that my soul is the whole of the World-Soul. Let us rise to the occasion, and vehemently declare that the Buddha, the World-Soul is part of My Soul, so that we should translate Baso's answer once more: "The Buddha—that is Your Mind!"

THE COMMENTARY

If you have grasped Baso's meaning, you are wearing Buddha's clothes, eating Buddha's food, speaking Buddha's words, doing Buddha's deeds, that is to say, you are Buddha himself. But though this may be so, Daibai has misled not a few people into mistaking the mark on the balance for the weight itself. He doesn't realize that if we explain the word "Buddha" we must rinse out our mouths for three days afterwards. If he had been a man of understanding, when he heard Baso say, "The mind is the Buddha," he would have covered his ears and rushed away.

In the Introduction to Case II of the *Hekiganroku* we have:

Say the word "Buddha," and you wallow in mud and flounder in puddles. Say the word "Zen," and your whole face is as red as a beetroot with shame and humiliation.

There is the famous story of *Eisen no mimi-arai*. The Emperor Gyo sent a messenger to a hermit named Kyoyu, offering to abdicate and hand over the Empire to him. Kyoyu not only flatly refused, but upon hearing such a filthy suggestion washed his ears in the river Ei. Another hermit, Sofu, coming there to water his ox, and seeing this, led his ox away, saying he would not let it drink such dirty water.

This kind of thing, strangely enough, is not to be found in Christianity. There is the word "religiosity" and "sanctimonious" as applied to particular people, but Zen feels sick with too much Zen. (The Zen) Buddha would like to have a rest sometimes, and swat flies and read a detective story and over-eat clotted cream.

THE VERSE

It is broad daylight, a fine day;
It is silly to rummage around,
And asking about the Buddha
Is like declaring oneself innocent while holding
  on to the stolen goods.

In the clear sky of Zen there is not a "Mind-is-Buddha" cloud. There is no need to search for truth or ask what the meaning of life is. If you have the thing in your pocket all the time, why should you say you haven't got it?

Mumon tells us that we are the Buddha—only we mustn't say so! Why not? Saying so makes the

144

Buddha something apart from ourselves, just as the words in the dictionary are apart from things. When we can speak a language, we don't need the book of words. When we live the Christian, the Buddhist, the Zen life, such phrases are meaningless. Telling us that our mind is the Buddha is like going out with someone who insists on telling us all the historical anecdotes of places and the botanical names of all the pretty weeds.

JOSHU'S OLD WOMAN

THE CASE

A monk of Joshu's asked an old woman the way to Taizan. She said, "Go straight on." After the monk had taken three or five steps, she said, "This monk also goes off like that." (He's just a common monk.) *Afterwards, another monk told Joshu about this, and Joshu said, "Wait a bit; I'll go and investigate this old lady for you." The next day off he went and asked the same question and got the same reply. On returning, Joshu said to the congregation of monks, "I've investigated the old lady of Taizan for you."*

With a smattering of Zen it is not difficult to make a fool of people. There seem to have been quite a number of old women who made themselves useful around the famous mountains (temples), pulling the legs of young monks. No doubt some of the old women were genuine, some not, and this is what Joshu "investigates."

The monk asks the way to the temple. The old woman answers as if he were asking about the Way, and tells him, as Stevenson says, "The way is straight like the grooves of launching," but the monk is quite oblivious of this, and thinks she is answering the plain, relative question in the plain, relative way. When the monk does not respond to her absolute answer, she sneers at him, out loud. Joshu conducts his investigation. Though he does not tell his monks the result, he cunningly suggests that he has found her out, in order to make a fool of them, for unless they become more foolish than they are already by birth they can never become clever.

In actual fact, the old woman's treating Joshu in exactly the same way as the young monk shows that her Zen was half-baked. If we love animals, we know who loves them and who not, but if we don't, we can't distinguish one from another. If we understand the music of Bach we also know those who understand it, and those who only pretend to. But this is not the point of the story, which is, *how* do you look at those who pretend to like animals and like Bach and like Zen? The feeling of superiority in such a case is a passport to Hell, or rather, it is Hell.

THE COMMENTARY

The old woman just sat still in her tent and planned the campaign; she didn't know that there was a famous bandit who knew how to take the enemy commander prisoner. Old Joshu was clever enough to steal into her camp and menace her fortress, but he wasn't a real general. Pondering over the matter, we must say that they both had their faults. Tell me now, what was Joshu's insight into the old woman?

Jimbo makes the story more coherent, and the military metaphor continuous, by translating it not as "a famous robber," but as "taking prisoner the enemy general," that is, "the old woman did not know how to take the enemy general (Joshu) prisoner." In any case, Mumon says that the old woman could defeat the young monks who passed by, but did not dare go to the temple and attack a master. At the end Mumon says rightly enough that there is something a bit measly about Joshu also, going sneaking round old women to see if their Zen was real or imitation. The impartiality of Mumon is miraculous.

THE VERSE

> *The question is the same.*
> *The answer is the same.*
> *Sand in the rice,*
> *Thorns in the mud.*

The question Joshu asked, "Is this the way to Taizan?" is the same that just all the monks asked. Her answer, "Straight ahead!" was the same for Joshu as for the silliest monk. Joshu's question, however, that looked like rice, had the sand of not-to-be-digested intellectual contradictions and paradoxes in it. What looked like mud, soft and easy, had in it the thorns of life upon which we fall and bleed.

From this Case we are to learn two things. First, not to do as Joshu did, investigate other people's Zen. Second, not to do as the old woman did, fail to distinguish the real Zen from the false, especially not to "entertain angels unaware."

BUDDHA AND THE
NON-BUDDHIST

THE CASE

A Non-Buddhist said to the Buddha, "I do not ask for words; I do not ask for silence." Buddha just sat quietly. The Non-Buddhist said admiringly, "The compassion of the World-Honored One has opened the clouds of my illusion, and has enabled me to enter on the Way." Making his salutations, he departed. Ananda then asked Buddha, "What was it this Non-Buddhist realized, that he so praised you?" The World-Honored One replied, "A high-class horse moves at even the shadow of the whip."

Logic is necessary when we are attempting to be logical, but this Non-Buddhist philosopher was not asking for logic. Thus when he requests Buddha to tell him something without speaking and without silence, and then Buddha is silent, he is not fool enough to object and charge Buddha with not fulfilling his demand. He gets what he wants, not something which is not speaking (that is silence) or speaking (i.e., not silence) but a Way. This Way is something which the historic Buddha was scarcely able to expound. It took more than another thousand years before Daruma and Eno

150

could point clearly to it. Further, in Buddha's thought, though not his experience, the world and the Way were divided—in fact we escape from one, existence, to the other, Nirvana. Zen is going back to the world with the touchstone in your pocket, so that the object of life is being achieved when we see things as they are, as bad as they can be and as good as they can be. This continuance of (our) suffering, Buddha relegated to the world, the flesh, and the devil. The continuance of (our) joy, Buddha kept for Nirvana, but Zen perceived that just as our joy and suffering are indivisible, so are Nirvana and the world, the absolute and the relative. Buddhism is thus always a duality, and Zen tends to fall into unity. This Way is what the Non-Buddhist received, not from the historical Buddha but from the Zen reunifying him with the world he rejected, so that the Buddha is not only the World-Honored One but a shit-stick and three pounds of flax, and the magnolia tree in the garden, and all the might-have-beens and mistakes and nightmares of mankind.

The simile of the horse comes from the *Zo Agongyo* where Buddha says there are four kinds of Bhiksu.

First there are horses that start even at the shadow of the whip, and perform the will of the horseman. Then there is one that does this when the hair is touched, another when the flesh is touched, and lastly one when the bone is touched. The first horse hears of the impermanence of another village; and feels world-nausea; the second feels it when he hears of the impermanence of his own village; the third when he hears of the impermanence of his own parents; and the fourth when he experiences illness and pain himself.

What the story teaches is the importance, above that of Zen itself, of the imagination. The Non-Buddhist had the imaginative power to see into the Buddha's state of mind and body when he sat there silent. In this sense, the most important thing for a man who wishes to study Zen, something he must do before he begins it, and must do with his last dying breath, is to cultivate his imagination. With imagination we have already some idea of the meaning of, for example, "When Buddha sat, all things sat." The Buddha's silence was not what we call "an eloquent silence." He was not hinting at something difficult to say. He was not suggesting that the question was unprofitable, or that the absolute was beyond (the relation of) speech and silence. His sitting there was no different from his walking, or going to the lavatory. There was no separation from himself and a leaf of a tree in the forests of the Amazon, or the fingernails of Julius Caesar.

What was the Non-Buddhist's illusion that Buddha cleared up? "If it be possible, let this cup pass from me." What was his enlightenment? "I and my cup are one."

As far as Ananda's childish question is concerned, some say he asked it for the sake of the other monks, others, Mumon among them, take it as a real inquiry on the part of Ananda.

THE COMMENTARY

Ananda was the Buddha's disciple, but his understanding was nothing like that of the Non-Buddhist. Just tell me, what is the difference between disciples and non-disciples?

"What is the difference between . . . ?" is a question Mumon likes to ask. It reminds one of the puzzle, "What is the difference between an elephant and a mail box?" If you answer, "I don't know," the retort is, "Then I won't ask you to mail a letter!" Once more, what is the difference between a disciple and a non-disciple? The answer is that the disciple may be the less understanding and faithful of the two. But the real question is: What is the difference between an enlightened man and an unenlightened man? If we say none, this goes against common sense, and common sense means God's sense. If we say they are as different as chalk and cheese, this denies the Buddha nature and the Fatherhood of God. The answer is that you don't know the difference until you realize yourself to be no better than others, then you are better than others. But if you think this, you are not. Here is the paradox that rules the world; here is the driver with his whip; can you see the shadow?

THE VERSE

> *Walking along the edge of a sword;*
> *Running over jagged ice;*
> *Not using a ladder;*
> *Climbing precipices handless.*

Zen often uses the feats of conjurors and acro-bats to express its mental-physical activities. Houdini, who used to enter, manacled, into a great jar of water, had much more Zen than many people think they have. The ice of the second line is taken as "smooth ice," "frozen ice," and also as "thin ice," which last gives the best meaning.

"Walking along the edge of a sword" is what we do every day, without knowing it. Death hovers over us, but we walk along what we suppose, rightly enough, to be a broad highway. As soon as we think about it, over we go, spiritually at least. When we forget ourselves, forget Zen, completely, no ice is too thin to pass over, that is to say, *if it will bear us,* but when we consider the (intellec-tual) alternatives, we are drowned on dry land, starved to death in a land of plenty, in this case without any "if" at all.

JOSHU'S OAK TREE

THE CASE

A monk asked Joshu, "What did Daruma come to China for?" Joshu answered, "The oak tree in the (temple) front garden."

The question, "What did Daruma bring to China and the world from India?" and, "What did Christ bring to Judea and the world from Heaven?" are very similar, but when for the answer we put the oak tree in the garden beside the lilies of the field, there is a great difference. To these we may add the flower that Buddha is supposed to have held up before the congregation of monks. Again, what was different in Christ's attitude of mind when he taught the disciples, "Our Father which art in Heaven," and when he pointed to the wildflowers? Let us transpose the words, and see how it feels. "Consider the Father, how he grows!" "Our Lily which art in Heaven!"

Where Buddhism and Christianity make their mistakes is not in experience, which is infallible, but in the analysis of it. This analysis affects the preceding experience and that is the (only) reason for its importance. Poetic and religious experience means SEEING SOMETHING (hearing, touch-

ing, smelling, and so on are included in "see").
This experience is also of its own validity, and
we are as certain of it as when we merely see something. But the moment we attempt, in either
case, to answer the question, "And WHAT did
you SEE," or, "And what did you see?" all is confusion. Note that the question may, and should
perhaps always be written, "Whom did what see?"
The confusion arises from the fact that what or
who is seen is not separable (except in words and
thought) from what or who sees, and the seeing is
not separable from the thing seen. When "I" and
the poetry or the truth, or my father, or the
flower, or the oak tree are set against each other,
both are meaningless. This is why Christ says, or
John says for him, "I and my Father are one," "Ye
shall be in me, and I in you," and so on. The trouble with Christians is that when they read "Christ
in you, the hope of glory," they understand it in
all its literality and transcendentalism, but the
moment they begin to explain it, it becomes a
metaphor, and "in," which means "equals," is
taken as "influencing."

The remarkable thing about this Case, which
Mumon has abbreviated, is that the monk also
makes the mistake of those who look for God outside themselves or inside themselves. The full account is as follows:

> A monk asked, "What is the meaning of the
> First Patriarch's coming from the West?" Joshu
> answered, "The oak tree in the front garden."
> The monk said, "Don't express it objectively!"
> Joshu replied, "I do not do so." The monk said,

"What is the meaning of the First Patriarch's coming from the West?" Joshu replied, "The oak tree in the front garden."

"Objectively" means with reference to an objective mental projection regarded as reality. When Joshu said, "The oak tree," when Buddha held up the flower, when Christ pointed to the lilies, when Tozan said, "Three pounds of flax," when Ummon said, "A shit-stick"—they were not dealing with external objects, any more than Hyakujo was speaking subjectively when, in answer to the question, "What is truth?" he answered, "Here I sit on Daiju Peak," or Christ when he declared, "I am the Light of the World," or Basho when he wrote:

> The cob ambles slowly
> Across the summer moor:
> I find myself in a picture.

THE COMMENTARY

If you grasp Joshu's answer clearly and strongly, there is for you no former Sakyamuni Buddha, or Maitreya Buddha to come.

When we know God, we don't need him, any more than the fish needs the water or the bird needs the air. Expressed violently, this is, "If you meet a Buddha in the street, kill him!" Expressed gently, Dosho says:

The green bamboos are all the Nyorai;
The melancholy yellow flowers—every one is
   Hannya. (Wisdom personified).

THE VERSE

Words do not express things;
Phrases do not show the mind-movement.
He who receives (only) words is lost;
To stagnate with sentences is to be deluded.

Words do not express things. Words express
words. Things are not expressed by words; things
express things. A thing and its word are two aspects of one Thing-Word. A thing without a word
is nothing. A word without a thing is nothing.
The (movement of the) mind is not expressed by
the body. The body expresses itself, just as the
mind expresses itself. But the mind and the body
are two aspects of one thing, as Blake said, and
Lawrence tried to put into practice.

Joshu said, "The oak tree in the front garden."
These are words, and you must not take the words
as pointing to the Truth. Or rather, let us say that
words, like trees, all point, but not at Truth. The
pointing is itself the Truth, just as the Name of
God is God himself.

To explain with a sentence is wrong. The sentence is itself the Truth. The finger points to the
moon. The finger is the reality, not the moon.
The moon is just the means for the finger to

point, which is the end. All this is not what Mumon says, and not quite what he means, but I have too much respect for Mumon and myself to suppose that he would disagree with me.

GOSO'S COW

THE CASE

A reddish yellow cow passes by a window. The head and horns and the four legs go past. Why doesn't the tail too?

This Case is the most troublesome of the forty-eight. What is the tail that remains behind? Dogen Zenji says of it:

> In this world,
> The cow's tail, that should come out
>   From the window,
> Always remains behind,
> Unless we pull it like mad.

The cow's tail is all that we cannot understand, all that we are incapable of. It is our desire to comprehend Zen, which belongs to the whole personality, with a part of it, the intellect. Only the whole can understand the whole, but this part, which is specifically human, and which has raised the insoluble problem, which is fated to try to accomplish this impossible task, has this destiny, to find out what its destiny is. The cow's tail, so to speak, pushes the cow from the dark cow-house through the window into the world of light and liberty, but itself, the questioning intellect, remains in its own darkness. Christ has been crucified for us, Socrates drank poison, Buddha reduced himself to skin and bone for our sakes, but the tail is still there. What a happy thing it is!

THE COMMENTARY

If in regard to this, you are able, even when in a hurry, to fix your one eye on it, and say a turning-word, you will be able to repay the Four Obligations and help the Three Bhava (all living creatures). *If you are still unable to do this, reflect again on the tail, and you can do it.*

Mumon is not telling us how to get the tail through the window, for in this fable, or dream, such a thing is impossible. Thoreau writes in his *Journal*, 1840:

> Make the most of your regrets; never smother your sorrow, but tend and cherish it until it comes to have a separate and integral interest. To regret deeply is to live afresh.

So Mumon tells us to meditate without ceasing on the cow's tail.

What is the object of life? Mumon suggests that it is not to become enlightened, or to go to Heaven, or do the will of God, or create beauty, or discover truth, or love one's neighbor, or be happy; but to return good for good, and save all men from their sin of dichotomizing. The first is Chinese; the second is what we may call, for once, Zen Buddhism. It is to the second that the tail belongs, for the tail is the hiatus between the Zen and the Buddhism, the real and the ideal.

THE VERSE

If the cow goes through, it will fall into a ditch;
If it goes back, it will be destroyed.
This little bit of a tail—
What a marvelous thing it is!

The commentators are all at sixes and sevens about this verse. Inoue says it is not the cow, but the tail, the remaining passion that will cause the man to fall into Hell. Jimbo says the first line refers to falling into the error of Emptiness, the second line to the mistake of Materialism. The other commentators are more than usually swindling. Perhaps we may take the verse as proposing Mumon's usual alternatives, of which we can choose neither, with the tail still wagging in the last two lines. The conclusion of the whole matter would then be this. We have to live between the relative and the absolute, in both at the same time. This can be done, and is done, insofar as we really live at all. But in spite of this, and in addition to this, there is the everlasting why, the eternal whither, the ever-to-be-asked and never-to-be-answered Question.

UMMON AND A MISTAKE

THE CASE

A monk once asked about "The radiance shines" and so on, but before he could finish the first line, Ummon interrupted him, and said, "Aren't these the words of Chosetsu Shusai?" The monk replied, "Yes, they are." Ummon said, "You made a slip of the tongue." Afterwards, Shishin brought the matter up, and said, "Tell me, how did the monk make a slip of the tongue?"

The "slip of the tongue" is the problem of this Case. Jimbo takes it as "hackneyed," and there seems to be a general consensus that Christ should not have quoted from the Old Testament or Confucius from the Book of Songs. What was wrong with the monk was not his quoting, somewhat pretentiously, a Zen verse, but the fact that he was born at all. Ummon, like many but not all clever people, was short-tempered and squelched the monk, perhaps for ever. Ninety-nine percent of the people in churches and temples should have the same treatment. They should be in pinball parlors and music halls, and then no one will want to tease them.

Emerson says that it is as difficult to appropriate

the words of another as to write them in the first place. The great fault of men, to parody Mencius, is that they are exhibitionists. The monk intended to show off his enlightenment and, of course, demonstrated the opposite. The words are the man, and though all language is of its nature imitative, each word we speak must be invented anew. Thoreau says, thinking of Ummon, and not the monk:

> The words of some men are thrown forcibly against you, and adhere like burrs.

THE COMMENTARY

If in regard to this episode you have grasped Ummon's unapproachable method, and know how the monk made his slip of the tongue, you are in a position to be a teacher of men and gods, but if you are not yet clear about it, you have not even saved yourself.

A teacher is an empty man, empty of cant, of unimportant "world events," of desiring and abhorring, of his own (and others') profit and loss. What does he teach? He communicates his own emptiness. He empties other people, in the perhaps foolish belief that,

> When the half-gods go
> The Gods arrive.

However, saving ourselves first and then other people is like the man who practices an E major sonata without the sharps, and then puts them in when he can play it perfectly. To save others is to save ourselves; to save ourselves is to save others—not only in some mysterious, transcendental, mystical I-am-you way, but because to teach is to learn and to learn is to teach.

THE VERSE

> *Angling in a swift stream—*
> *Greedy for the bait, he is caught!*
> *You have only to open your mouth,*
> *And your life is lost!*

"The swift stream" is said to refer to the suddenness of Ummon's interrupting the monk in his quotation. "Greedy for the bait" refers to the monk's anxiety to be enlightened, which, being too great, results in frustration. Here is the necessity of what Basho in his later years called *karumi*, lightness, a kind of humor, or smiling. Love without humor begins and ends in tragedy, as Shakespeare clearly shows us, but Zen without humor! Here is a stink indeed.

DARUMA'S MIND-PACIFYING

THE CASE

Daruma sat facing the wall. The Second Patriarch, having cut off his arm, stood there in the snow. He said, "Your disciple's mind has no peace as yet. I beg the Teacher to give it rest." Daruma replied, "Bring your mind here and I will give it rest." The Patriarch said, "I have searched for that mind, and have not found it." Daruma said, "Then I have put it to rest."

Mumon has abbreviated the case here, almost to incomprehensibility to anyone reading it for the first time. The account given in the *Dentoroku*, however, is detailed to the point of incredibility. It tells us that Eka stood there in the snow on December the 9th until the falling snow reached his knees, and then Daruma, taking compassion on him (if he had not, it would have reached his ears), asked what he wanted. Eka, with tears running down his face, said this and that, and Daruma said this and that, and then Eka cut off his left arm with a sword and laid it before Daruma, and Daruma said this and that, and then we have the present Case. It is not recorded what they did with the arm.

There is an odd similarity between the transmission-enlightenment of the first three patriarchs from Daruma:

Sosan: "Cleanse me from my sins."
Eka: "Bring them here and I will cleanse you."
Sosan: "I have sought for them, but could not find them."
Eka: "Then I have cleansed you."

Doshin: "Open the gate of release for me!"
Sosan: "Who has constrained you!"
Doshin: "No one constrains me."
Sosan: "Then why do you ask for release?"

The interesting point about the present Case is the way in which the quietism and negativism of early Zen, which was still Indian-flavored, changed to activism and positivism from the Sixth Patriarch, who told Emyo to find his real nature, his nature before he was born. Not to be able to find the self, and to be able to find the Self, is the same thing; also it is of course different.

THE COMMENTARY

The broken-toothed old foreigner crossed the sea importantly from a hundred thousand miles away. This was raising waves when there is no wind. Daruma had only one disciple, and even he was a cripple. Well, well!

"Raising waves where there is no wind" is a favorite expression in Zen, signifying that there is no problem of life. Things are as they are, and as they are becoming, and once you realize this in its active, not resigned, meaning, there is nothing really to worry about. Further, our ordinary way of thinking about life in general is like an ingrowing toenail. And last, the Buddhas and the Patriarchs of Zen are doctors who cause the disease they pretend to cure. So, since this is the best of all possible worlds, why all this fuss about Daruma and Eka and the *Mumonkan?* From this comes Ikkyu's famous doka:

> Since that mischievous creature
> Called Sakya
> Was born into this world,
> How many, many people
> Have been befooled!

Zen has much in common with Panglossism, but this is balanced by the abuse of Buddha and the Patriarchs. In Western culture we find this freedom only in the history of the Rationalists, where it has almost always been accompanied by a complete lack of poetry, not to speak of religious feeling. Almost the best thing about Zen is the way in which it releases in us both the freedom of the radical and the faith and devotion of piety.

THE VERSE

Coming from the West, and direct pointing—
All the trouble comes from this!
The jungle of monks being all at sixes and sevens
Comes from these two chaps.

Many people have believed in all seriousness
what Mumon says jokingly, that religion has been
a curse to humanity. However, man is a religious
animal, just as he is a cowardly, brave, wise, foolish, patient, irritable animal. Further, just as we
cannot have peace without (the possibility of) war,
so we cannot have religion without irreligion, or,
as the Verse above says, all the problems of the
meaning of Daruma's coming from the West, and
pacifying Eka's mind, and not finding that mind,
or finding the Mind—all these things come from
inanition and Buddhist peace and animal apathy.
Thus Mumon's irony is justified in that Zen,
though the greatest creation of mankind, is at the
same time its growing pains, the inadvertent but
inevitable cause of religious mania, masochism,
persecution, fruitless asceticism and other less agreeable things in human history.